how to ~~have a~~ brilliant career
without ever having a proper job

> *Job security is gone forever. The time is right for ambitious individuals to take control of their own careers.*

> *Break out of the cosy corporation and build a career on your own terms.*

how to have a brilliant career
without ever having a proper job

AN **ACTIVE** GUIDE TO SELF-EMPLOYMENT

Stuart Crainer

PITMAN PUBLISHING
128 Long Acre, London WC2E 9AN

A Division of Pearson Professional Limited

First published in Great Britain 1995

© Stuart Crainer 1995

British Library Cataloguing in Publication Data
A CIP catalogue record for this book can be obtained from the British Library.

ISBN 0 273 61175 5

All rights reserved; no part of this publication may be reproduced, stored in a retrieval system, or transmitted in any form or by any means, electronic, mechanical, photocopying, recording, or otherwise without either the prior written permission of the Publishers or a licence permitting restricted copying in the United Kingdom issued by the Copyright Licensing Agency Ltd, 90 Tottenham Court Road, London W1P 9HE. This book may not be lent, resold, hired out or otherwise disposed of by way of trade in any form of binding or cover other than that in which it is published, without the prior consent of the Publishers.

10 9 8 7 6 5 4 3 2 1

Typeset by Northern Phototypesetting Co. Ltd, Bolton
Printed and bound in Great Britain by Bell and Bain Ltd, Glasgow

The Publishers' policy is to use paper manufactured from sustainable forests.

Contents

1 The changing world of work — 1
Facing up to tomorrow's world today — 1
Meeting the new challenge — 3
Inside the corporation — 4
The proper job — 8
Taking control of your career — 9
The brilliant career — 13
Achieving a balance — 15
Why leave the cosy corporation? — 17
Why work for yourself? — 19
Health, wealth and happiness — 21
Pros and cons of self-employment — 24

2 Making a start — 27
Seven steps — 27
Step 1: Thinking — 27
Step 2: Questioning — 36
Step 3: What's the big idea? — 37
Step 4: Testing — 47
Step 5: Timing — 53
Step 6: Creating — 56
Step 7: Starting — 61
Planning your start — 64

3 What skills do you need?   67
Intuition   71
Decision-making   75
Communication   80
Selling   82
Marketing   90
Negotiating   96
Sweat and obsession   99

4 Managing the money   103
The financial obstacle course   103
Money for starters   106
Sources of support   110
Dealing with the tax man   113
Do you need to be VAT registered?   117
Focused finance   118
The route to financial fiasco   125

5 Where you work   129
The death of the office   132
The office at home   135
Using technology   138

6 People and your business   145
The family comes too   145
People just don't understand   146
Managing stress   147
Managing your time   150
Managing people   156

Learning to delegate ... 163
Leading people ... 166

7 Making your business work ... 171
Developing your business ... 171
Remember who you are in business for ... 173
Get close to customers ... 174
Turn customers into advocates ... 179
Become partners with suppliers ... 187
Keep it simple ... 189
Commit to quality ... 191
Watch the competition ... 192
Spread the burden ... 194
Use experts ... 196
Develop systems and processes ... 198
Develop skills ... 202
Recruit people professionally ... 203
Seize the opportunity ... 205
Develop and use networks ... 208
Make the most of publicity ... 208
Go for it! ... 210

Index ... 212

"Change is now endemic in the business world ... In such a climate, people must change their attitudes, skills and behaviour if they are to survive and prosper"

The changing world of work

● Facing up to tomorrow's world today

Look in the dictionary under 'career' and you will find something similar to *moving fast and uncontrollably*. Working careers can feel just like that. Opportunities come up and then quickly disappear. As your career propels itself forward it can seem as if it is out of control and that the last person who has any say in it is yourself. Moving off the career track can seem drastic. Who wants to get off something which is fast moving? It is risky. Why choose an alternative when you're well paid and secure in the knowledge that the monthly salary cheque will arrive? Is it an admission of failure, that you can't cope with the hurly burly of corporate existence?

Recent years have seen huge reductions of employees in most large organisations. Through redundancy many people have been forced to reappraise their careers. Once brilliant careers have stalled. Traditional, secure, 'proper' jobs have decreased in numbers and, perhaps as importantly, in the opportunities they provide. The days of a job for life and steady progression up a career ladder have gone. Many full-time jobs have simply disappeared. This is happening throughout the developed world. From 1992 to 1993 the US economy grew by 2.6 per cent. This apparently signalled the end of recession and seemed to be good news. For many people it undoubtedly was good news but, at the same time as the economy started to grow again, over 500,000 clerical and technical positions disappeared, probably for good. Many jobs just no longer exist.

Of course, we have all witnessed the disappearance of many traditional jobs. Shipbuilders and miners are nearing extinction – joining a lengthy list including the men with red flags in front of cars, horse dung collectors, hangmen, scribes, music hall entertainers and stone wall builders. This time, however, the changes are more far reaching. In particular, jobs in management have been made redundant on a huge scale. A swathe has been cut through what was once the safest place in the business world – middle management.

A survey by *3i* in the United Kingdom found that early in 1994 – again after the worst of recession was supposedly over – two-thirds of companies expected a further reduction in middle management numbers. In a survey of 50 top UK companies in 1993, recruitment company Cedar International found that a massive 86 per cent had implemented redundancies in the previous year and, in addition, 36 per cent were operating rolling programmes spanning a number of years involving a significant proportion of the workforce.

You don't need to refer to research to discover the extent of the changes now under way. Take a typical day's news. Today is 11th November 1994: Royal Insurance forecasts a 10 per cent reduction in its workforce over the next three years in spite of tripling profits; BT announces it is on course to reduce its numbers by 15,000 during the year; and Ladbrokes is to reduce its head office and central staff by more than half. This is the news from a single day and it is only the big names which make the news. Countless other companies are making similar, less heralded announcements.

The brutal truth is that technology enables companies to do more work with less people. The successful companies of the future, says management guru Charles Handy, will be able to employ half as many people paid twice as much to produce three times what they now produce. Cynics might observe that companies have, so far, missed out the middle element while trying to achieve the others. The trend towards flatter and leaner organisations looks set to continue for the foreseeable future. Technology moves ceaselessly forward and, equally importantly, companies are becoming more adept at using technology to work more flexibly and quickly. Tomorrow may literally find any group of workers made redundant.

The message is clear. Change is now endemic in the business world. It doesn't matter what the business is or where it is located, but it will be affected by continuing processes of change – technological change; changes in markets, products and services; changes in the expectations of employees; and change in many other manifestations. In such a climate, people must change their attitudes, skills and behaviour if they are to survive and prosper. For many the solution to all these challenges is self-employment.

● Meeting the new challenge

Forging your own brilliant career is not easy. There are substantial risks in starting your own business, but self-employment is something an increasing number of people are turning to. Instead of allowing organisations to dictate their careers they are creating their own through self-employment or more flexible working arrangements.

It is estimated that there are around 2.9 million people in the United Kingdom who are either owners of small firms or who are self-employed. Self-employment nearly doubled in the 1980s – by the end of the decade one in eight of the working population were self-employed. Of these, women accounted for more than a quarter (compared to a fifth in 1979). An increasing proportion of new entrants to self-employment were people under 35, with an even sharper increase among the under 25s. This suggests that the people starting and running small businesses are becoming younger.

This is not yet another short-lived trend. In fact, the old ways of work are fast disappearing. As many as 38 per cent of Britain's workers are no longer in full-time employment. Instead, around 9.7 million people are either part-timers, in temporary jobs, self-employed, on a government training scheme or are unpaid family workers, a rise of 1.25 million since 1986.

● Inside the corporation

Why are all these people fleeing from the traditional lure of *proper* jobs inside comfortable and reassuringly large corporations? Clearly, some have had no choice. They have been made redundant or have seen the writing on the wall and left. A survey of 700 small firms by the National Federation of Enterprise Agencies and *The Observer* newspaper identified the single most important factors in deciding to set up your own business as:

- Desire to run your own business   36%
- Redundancy   27%
- No jobs available   18%
- More freedom to make decisions   7%
- Good business idea   6%
- Desire to make money   6%

> **"Technological progress means that many people no longer have a role to play in conventional organisations."**

Technological progress means that many people no longer have a role to play in conventional organisations. For those at the sharp end, redundancy is a traumatic and unsettling experience. Many people believed their jobs were safe or their employer was committed to finding them jobs elsewhere in the organisation. Often they have been disappointed and have had to contemplate new working lives for themselves.

As people head off towards the unknown – whether voluntarily leaving the corporate world or as a result of redundancy – they might like to look over their shoulders at those who remain with the company. Having done so, they are likely to feel a lot better about their situation. For those who remain within organisations the demands of work are liable to increase. There will be fewer people to turn to (or blame) and the emphasis will be on continually enhancing skills.

Despite technology, working with organisations has, in fact, never been more demanding and stressful. According to the 1993 Institute of Management (IM) report, *Managers Under Stress*, managers are working long hours and their workload is increasing – 41 per cent work at least 50 hours a week; 13 per cent more than 60 hours; 75 per cent reported that their workload had increased over the previous year and 35 per cent calculated it rose by at least a third. In her book *The Overworked American*, Juliet Smof found that the average employed American now works 164 more hours a year than 20 years ago – the equivalent of an extra month. Clearly, this is not the leisure age.

Of course, work also brings with it a great deal of stress which affects all aspects of people's lives. The IM research, covering nearly 1,000 managers, looked into the extent of work-related anxiety:[1]

	Very anxious (%)	Anxious (%)	Not anxious (%)
Future employment			
Lack of further career opportunities	25	50	25
Possibility of redundancy	16	55	29
Lack of job security	21	55	24
Possible age discrimination	24	38	38
Work – family issues			
Demands of work on relationship with family	20	57	23
Demands of work on relationship with partner	21	53	26
Demands of the job			
Ability to fulfil role	4	35	61
Not having the right skills	4	41	55
Lack of training	5	43	52
Meeting targets/deadlines	8	58	34

[1] *Managers Under Stress*, Institute of Management, Corby, 1993

Conflicting demands on work time	19	63	18
Financial concerns			
Money shortages	17	52	31
Mortgage repayments	9	38	53
Pension arrangements	13	47	40

Note: Percentages may not total 100 due to rounding.

This research seems to show that it is not so much the content and nature of the work which causes anxiety and stress, but the ramifications of change and fears for the future.

It appears likely that the pace of change will continue to accelerate. There will be no respite. Nor can those people who remain with the corporation anticipate the solace and encouragement of regular promotions. In the future, promotions will be few and far between. IBM UK chairman, Sir Anthony Cleaver, announced that his organisation was reducing its number of management tiers to a mere four. This, said Cleaver, 'means a maximum of one promotion every ten years and even this is for the one man who makes it to the top'. The others in the organisation can no longer rely on moving steadily up the corporate ladder – the rungs are now so wide apart that only a few will be able to stretch their legs enough to climb.

Those who plan to join the upwardly mobile and still believe in neat and well-ordered career structures are likely to be disappointed. The IM tracked the career development of over 800 UK managers from 1980 to 1992. It found that sideways or downwards moves among managers more than doubled during the period from 7 per 100 managers in 1980–1982 to nearly 15 per 100 in 1992. 'As the pace of change accelerates, the idea of a progressive career within stable organisational structures is increasingly threatened,' says the IM report on the research. 'The structures which have traditionally supported rational long-term careers are being gradually replaced with more fluid organisations.' And it is people who are the most fluid of corporate resources.

The impression of instability is emphasised by the IM's findings that managers are changing jobs more often. They are job hopping in search of better jobs, often not on their own terms, but increasingly because of corporate restructuring. In the 1980s managers tended to change jobs for proactive reasons – personal and career development – in the 1990s they are often reacting to change which has been imposed on them, whether redundancy or relocation. Among the 800 managers included in the survey, 25 per cent of those who changed jobs in 1992 did so because of reorganisation – in the early 1980s the figure was eight per cent. These dramatic changes in managerial career development pose questions which strike at the heart of Western managerial culture. 'Young managers were once shown career structures stretching ten or even 15 years ahead. Stay with us and this is where you can go, they were told. Companies simply can't say that now,' says Bill Hudson, one of the managers in the report.

For managers at the sharp end, the changing structure of careers is not easily understood. 'In the 1980s you could plan your career. There were a lot of opportunities. Now, you have to accept that the only way is not always up,' says a redundant manager who recently applied for a job working for someone he once managed. Strangely, the insecurity has not yet transmitted itself to some managers. Trudy Coe, co-author of the IM survey, says: 'Managers have to be prepared and, at the moment, many appear complacent. They think their careers are safe.'

Research carried out by the IM in 1992 found that 40 per cent of managers anticipated that their next career move would be upwards. Such optimism flies in the face of reality. Managers – and many others – need to look at their careers differently. They have to see sideways moves as an opportunity to develop the broad portfolio of skills they now need. In the past people looked to organisations to shape their careers and skills for them, now the onus is on them. They need to be prepared for change and to recognise its potential benefits rather than regarding it as a threat.

● The proper job

A traditional *proper*, and *ideal*, job may well have followed this pattern:

Age	Corporate position
Early 20s	Join company as a trainee manager
Mid 20s	Promoted/relocated
Late 20s	Assistant head of department
Early 30s	Head of department
Mid 30s	Promoted/relocated to become head of division
Early 40s	Promoted to the board
Late 40s	Become managing director
Mid 50s	Become chairman
Late 50s	Retire

Most people don't reach the dizzy executive heights of chairman, managing director or even a director. Their careers tend to reach a plateau – they become head of a particular division or department and then remain there. And the longer they remain with a single company in a particular position the more likely it is that their skills are no longer useful or transferable to another organisation. They are stuck.

An Inland Revenue leaflet sums up the *proper* job. According to the IR, if you answer 'yes' to the following, you are probably employed:

- *Do you yourself have to do the work rather than hire someone else to do it for you?*

- *Can someone tell you at any time what to do or when and how to do it?*

- *Are you paid by the hour, week or month? Can you get overtime pay?*

- *Do you work set hours, or a given number of hours a week or month?*

- *Do you work at the premises of the person you work for, or at a place or places he or she decides?*

Even if you answer 'yes' to these questions, creating your own brilliant career may be more accessible than it now appears.

● Taking control of your career

Step 1: Make the time

Taking control of your career is not easy. Time is at a premium and managing the future is secondary when coping with the present is so demanding. People are under daily pressure to deliver results – no matter what their job or where they work. People have to move fast so there is little time for them to step outside the organisation and review their career.

The first step, therefore, is to make the time. If you don't know where your career is going in the short to medium term, how can you manage it effectively? If you don't make the time you will never know what you are doing, where you are going and, perhaps, what you are missing.

Step 2: Find someone to talk to

It is important at all stages in this process to remember that you aren't alone.

The obvious internal source of support in an organisation is the personnel department. Though they can be helpful they are, by their very position, part of the organisation. It is, therefore, very hard for internal IR or personnel people to give an objective view of the possible paths your career could take. If you are part of a company appraisal system, this might offer another way forward. However, conventional appraisal systems have often proved unable to cope with the continual tide of change. Typically, an organisation can find that when it comes to a year-end appraisal of managers' performance half have either moved elsewhere in the company or have left. This makes it almost impossible for internal departments to keep abreast of the career and development needs of individuals.

With objective and up-to-date views difficult to find within the organisation, it might be useful to turn to external consultants for one-to-one career counselling. This is something an increasing number of organisations are using. The personal approach is most obviously useful when managers are made redundant. However, it clearly has potential benefits for those still in work who are unsure as to the direction of their careers or which skills they will need in the future. Of course, the catch for employers is that the consultants may well be advising managers that their next move should be elsewhere. In some cases companies bring in career counsellors when they are looking to make people redundant; one-to-one counselling helps identify who really wants and needs to work elsewhere and who are the people who would benefit themselves and the organisation by staying.

One manager who benefited from the one-to-one approach is Bill Harris. Made redundant by Westland in 1992, he worked together with Coutts Career Consultants to examine his future career possibilities. Coutts' counselling programme for senior managers is labelled as a 'safe house', time for managers to review – in confidence – their career to date and develop and assess their future direction. Bill Harris cites career counselling as the major factor in his decision to become a self-employed consultant after a career in large organisations.

'The range of career alternatives open to me was diminishing,' he says. 'The career counselling enabled me to take stock of myself and my career. If you have spent your career working for a company you are concerned with the day-to-day business of managing rather than thinking about what kind of person you are or what kind of skills you have. I hadn't actually thought about running my own business before and thought I was destined to continue as a corporate career man.

The counselling convinced me I had what it takes to succeed by myself. It provided powerful reinforcement and support.'
Bill Harris is now established as an independent management consultant based on the Isle of Wight.

Step 3: What are your strengths and weaknesses?

Having made the time – even a few hours thinking about what you would like to do is a start, and may even be enough – you have to be able to look at your strengths and weaknesses in an objective way. This is something most of us are unused to and not necessarily very good at. Indeed, you may have to break the habits of a life-time. Traditionally, self-analysis has not been a prerequisite for career success.

Taking control of your career involves two basic skills:

- **Insight**   You have to have a realistic view of your own strengths and limitations. This is something people are often particularly poor at – they don't know what their strengths are and where they would be best used.

- **Being proactive**   No-one else is going to do it for you. You have to actively seek out opportunities and be prepared to take personal risks. Talented people have always taken their development and careers seriously. They know their strengths and where they would be best utilised.

Successful people – no matter what their occupation – tend to have a happy knack of being in the right place at the right time all the time. They are adept at using their skills where they are needed most. This appears to be commonsense – after all Manchester United doesn't play Ryan Giggs as a defender; surgeons don't answer the telephone. But in many companies people's strengths aren't played to – or sometimes even recognised. Taking hold of your career must begin with an awareness of yourself. What suits you? What do you enjoy and what are you good at?

> **"Self-awareness is the key to successful career management. You need to realise that you have to learn."**

Of course, coming to terms with your strengths also involves accepting gaps in your knowledge and experience. In reality, a lot of people are more interested in papering over the cracks rather than harnessing their capabilities. People aren't comfortable with failure and regard admitting to development needs as a sign of weakness rather than something which is positive and that will have long-term benefits. Accepting that you are far from perfect and do not possess every single skill and ability that your working life requires, demands a degree of humility. We know we are not perfect, but we tend to leave it at that. Self-awareness is the key to successful career management. You need to realise that you have to learn. For many people this means that they have to learn how to learn.

This is a major stumbling block. Apparently successful people have often built their experience and instincts around implementation and are poorly equipped to recognise when, what and how they are learning. They are good at doing things rather than pondering on what they learned as they did them and how this is useful.

● The brilliant career

Careers are now taking on a myriad of different patterns – though the proper job with its plateau remains dominant. A brilliant career might follow the following pattern:

The stages of learning

Learning a new skill you pass through a number of stages:

- **Unconscious incompetence**   You don't know you can't do it.
- **Conscious incompetence**   You know what you can't do.
- **Conscious competence**   You are aware that you are doing it.
- **Unconscious competence**   You do it without thinking.

Age	Corporate position/self-employed
Early 20s	Join company as trainee manager
Mid 20s	Experience with a variety of business units
Late 20s	International experience; emphasis on building up contacts and skills
Early 30s	Take time out (supported by the company) to study
Mid 30s	Head of international business unit
Late 30s	Become self-employed, initially offering your expertise as a consultant to your former employer
Early 40s	Develop own business

Late 40s	Take on more staff and partners to delegate greater managerial responsibility
Early 50s	Start another business in an area of personal interest
Late 50s	Contemplate retiring but decide simply to cut down working a little.

This, inevitably, is an optimistic scenario. But it gives some idea of the range of experience and skills which will be increasingly critical in managing your own brilliant career. Overcoming the plateau, so that your skills and experience are continually developed and enhanced, is critical to success.

Consultant and author, Tim Foster, has managed to forge his own unique career. Periods of self-employment in the 1970s and 1980s have been punctuated by spells with large organisations. Like a growing number of people, he has called the shots rather than dodging the bullets in the corporate rifle range. In mapping out their own futures many others will follow a similar path.

According to the Inland Revenue, if you can answer 'yes' to the following questions, it will usually mean you are self-employed:

- *Do you have the final say in how the business is run?*
- *Do you risk your own money in the business?*
- *Are you responsible for meeting the losses as well as taking the profits?*
- *Do you provide the main items of equipment you need to do your job, not just the small tools many employees provide for themselves?*
- *Are you free to hire other people on your own terms to do the work you have taken on? And do you pay them out of your own pocket?*

- Do you have to correct unsatisfactory work in your own time and at your own expense?

If you work in an organisation and can't answer 'yes' to these questions, think of the changes in your life if you did work for yourself and could answer 'yes'.

● Achieving a balance

'Work is more than a job', says Charles Handy. 'In the past, business was the employer of all those who wanted to work. In the future there will be lots of customers, but not lots of jobs.' To Handy the future world of work will follow, what he calls, the 'doughnut principle'. 'Organisations have their essential core of jobs and people surrounded by an open and flexible space which they fill with flexible workers and flexible supply contracts,' he says. Handy argues that organisations have neglected and misunderstood the core while expanding and developing the rest of the doughnut. He attaches the same image to people's personal development, suggesting that many need to sit down and return to first principles if they are to achieve a balance in their lives.

The trouble is that balance is notoriously elusive. Frenzied commuters may feel totally drained by the morning train journey, but they usually shrug their shoulders and reflect that their salary makes it worthwhile. The self-employed may miss the routine of actually travelling to work. The novelty of walking upstairs to the office while dodging the clutter of toys and side-stepping family debris may quickly pall. But a balance can be achieved. Charles Handy actually practises what he preaches. He has, what he labels, a portfolio. He writes, teaches and works with a variety of organisations. He also spends time abroad.

Others in the same business have a similar approach. Management consultant Richard Pascale is internationally renowned for his work and is paid by some of the world's leading corporations to advise them. His life appears highly stressful and demanding. He manages an interview over breakfast at seven o'clock in the morning. It is interrupted by the chauffeur of a chairman of a major company – the chairman is in a car outside asking whether Mr Pascale can travel with him to the airport to provide advice and reassurance. Yet, despite such demands on his time and energy, Pascale balances his life with extreme care and has managed to do so for a lengthy period. 'As I was finishing my MBA at Harvard, my colleagues were frantically searching for the "perfect" job. I found myself troubled by the process and unable to engage in it with enthusiasm,' he recalls. 'Then, one day I had an epiphany – what I really wanted to do was spend a quarter of my life teaching; a quarter consulting (to test the relevance of theory in practice); a quarter writing (something I enjoy – and when you put your ideas on paper you discover the holes in the logic); and, finally, a quarter of my life on holiday (to recreate). I have endeavoured to achieve that balance ever since.' Richard Pascale knows what he enjoys, knows what he is good at and knows which of his interests is liable to make the most money. He achieves a balance.

Sceptics might say that it is alright for highly paid management consultants to create a portfolio, but impossible for mere mortals with decidedly limited amounts of money, weighty mortgages and skills that are difficult to see being sold elsewhere.

It can be done. The revolution at work falls into two categories:

- People who have more flexible working arrangements – such as job sharing or working from home – but who still work for an organisation. The Henley Centre for Forecasting estimates that 15 per cent of work in the United Kingdom will be performed remotely by 1995.

- Those who have cut the corporate apron strings and have struck out for themselves.

Increasingly, the divide between the two is becoming hazy. Managers, for example, are now made redundant but are subsequently retained as consultants. Similarly, organisations are 'outsourcing' many of their activities to external organisations. Instead of doing everything in-house, they rely on external experts and specialists to supply their skills if, and when, they are required.

Outsourcing began life as something organisations did to their technical or peripheral functions. IT departments, for example, were outsourced as were other non-core activities such as catering, cleaning and security. Now outsourcing is affecting what were once central activities, such as personnel departments and accounts. The onus is on flexibility and being able to adapt to rapidly changing circumstances.

If these trends carry on – and all the experts seem to think they will – then the number of self-employed people will continue to grow. What's more, being self-employed will become the perfectly acceptable norm for many jobs and businesses throughout industry.

● Why leave the cosy corporation?

Things are rarely perfect – especially in the world of work. But for whatever reason, you have weighed up the pros and cons and made the decision to go it alone. There are pitfalls to cutting the corporate apron strings and some of the most basic include:

- ● *Success is not guaranteed* With any business there is a substantial risk of failure. No matter how much money you have and how much market research you do, your business may fail. The history of business is littered with great ideas which people didn't want. The Sinclair C5 may have been an innovative idea, but people simply weren't prepared to buy it.

- ● *Losing the safety net* From being cosseted by the corporation you are suddenly left performing without a safety net. You can no longer blame others or watch as the buck stops somewhere else. The buck stops and starts with you.

What's important to you?

Financial rewards

Think about your salary, your bonus and other perks.

Do you think they will continue to increase?

How much money do you *need* to earn?

Do you *need* the top-of-the-range car or the holiday in Hawaii sales bonus?

Family

Would you like to spend more time with your family?

How can you make that feasible?

Job satisfaction

How would you rate your current level of job satisfaction?

Are your skills being developed?

What do you enjoy about your job?

Will it continue?

What don't you enjoy about your job?

Will it continue?

- **Losing the corporate network**   Sometimes when people remove themselves from their organisations they find that their network of contacts disappears. Organisations provide their own hierarchical and tidy networks – people you can turn to for help and information. You may rely on them to a greater degree than you realise.

● Why work for yourself?

The attractions of self-employment are numerous – though they may not appear so as one cash flow crisis leads to another. Here are just some of the reasons to work for yourself.

- **Freedom**   'Self-employment brings a large amount of personal freedom. You don't have to dress up in a suit and if you want to sit down and play the piano you can do.' says Tim Foster. Being self-employed means you decide when you work and who you work for. This is true, but it is also worth remembering that success usually involves working long hours and, in the beginning, you will probably have little choice in who your customers are. There is freedom, but it is not unconditional.

- **Life-style**   For many people, self-employment is becoming a life-style decision. This means any number of things to different people, but usually includes some element of getting out of the rat race. This may involve spending more time with your children or moving from the city to the countryside.

- **Money**   Of course money is key. It is an important motivator for virtually everyone (even though they may protest otherwise). Some people who decide to become self-employed may believe that they can earn more money working for themselves. Realistically few small businesses grow into big businesses. But millions of people earn comfortable livings from small businesses ... some make millions. Alternatively, others believe that earning less money will be compensated for by additional freedom.

- **Escape** Not all reasons to become self-employed are positive. Many people simply decide that they have had enough of the company politics attached to working in any organisation and particularly large ones. They are heartily sick of the office gossip and want to escape to a world free from constant competition and pointless power games.

- **Independence and responsibility** People are often attracted by the simple fact that they will no longer be answerable to anyone else. If they make a mistake, the blame is laid fairly and squarely on their own shoulders. Sally McLeod worked in the National Health Service before becoming an independent consultant. 'I was frustrated with the work I was doing. I felt it didn't give me enough scope and I couldn't really see the results,' she says. 'Working as a consultant is fundamentally different – you can devote all your energy to a single project with a finite life-span. You are not side-tracked and you see the results of your work.'

After a year in business, Chris Thorpe's consultancy had a client base of 15 companies, including British Telecom, Glaxo and other multinationals. It achieved an international quality standard certificate within 18 months. There are, he admits, pitfalls to going it alone. 'Independence brings with it irregular income and working hours; an initial reduction in business contacts; the need to separate your business and personal life; realisation of who will support you and, finally, that success or failure is completely down to you.' Undeterred, he observes: 'I have found it a breath of fresh air. Consultancy allows you to become really involved with the client so that you become an extension of their department. You can undertake and complete a range of projects at the same time.'

It always helps to put down on paper the pros and cons as you see them. So think about why you want to become self-employed. Ensure, as much as you can, that your reasons are positive rather than negative.

You need to seek out constructive criticism wherever you can find it. Now, show what you have written to someone else – do they agree? If they do agree, ask them to give reasons. For example, if you want to become self-employed and run a pub and feel that now is the right time, they may elaborate and say that you have the correct skills: compatibility with many people, interest in people, talkative, etc. If they don't agree, ask them to give reasons. For example, running a pub in a new location may not be such a good idea without the extensive network of your family and friends nearby. You might have secretly acknowledged this to yourself, but put it to the back of your mind until the concern is raised by a friend.

● Health, wealth and happiness

The reality of the business world can seem weighed down with pessimism. If a good idea is to be turned into a good business the man or woman behind it must cast aside dismal forecasts and create their own optimistic scenario. There is a lot of idealism attached to starting up your own business. It may be the biggest risk (personally and financially) you ever take. Having a mortgage may feel a heavy burden, but consider a mortgage and possibly a number of employees relying on you for their monthly cheque to support their families.

Most people who go into business have an idea that to some degree they might achieve wealth, health and happiness – and not necessarily in that order. Among many other qualities there has to be a lot of the dreamer in the self-employed man or woman.

There are plenty of recipes for success. But for every neat and catchy success formula there are hundreds of business failures: good ideas which bit the corporate dust; bad ideas which predictably failed. Self-employment is not a cure-all.

Why do you want to become self-employed?

1

2

3

4

5

Indeed, one survey by the Institute of Manpower Studies found that a self-employed person is more than three times as likely to be in the poorest tenth of the workforce than an employee.[2]

Things do and will go wrong. According to research carried out by CCN Business Information nearly a quarter of all company directors in the United Kingdom have been involved with companies that have failed during the past six years. More than 10 per cent of these directors have had more than one failure and 1,000 have been involved in more than ten failed companies. So, for every impressive success story you read about there are many other failed businesses.

But all is not doom and gloom. Think of the following brilliant careers.

- **Anita Roddick,** Body Shop founder; a woman in a man's world and determinedly unconventional; now there is hardly a High Street without a Body Shop.

- **Richard Branson,** colourful jumpers and a flair for publicity belie the fact that with no experience of airlines he created a multi-million pound and very successful business.

- **Henry Ford,** a one-time boy racer with an apparently insane idea about everyone owning a car; soon many did and he made them.

- **Henry Heinz,** sold products from his garden aged five; bankrupt at 31; began again and soon had 57 varieties and more.

- **Percy Shaw,** a self-educated road repairer, he invented cat's eyes, soon produced 500,000 a year and became a millionaire (though never invested in carpets or curtains).

- **Charles Forte,** famously started commercial life with a milk bar and developed a nice little business.

---

[2] *Self-employment and the Distribution of Income*, Institute of Manpower Studies, Brighton, 1994

But it is better to be realistic and not imagine that you're about to make your million. Instead, draw up a list and decide upon what is important to you.

● Pros and cons of self-employment

Pros	Cons
● Independence	● Dependence on customers, suppliers, employees, etc
● Excitement of risk-taking	● Insecurity
● Stress of your own making	● A new sort of stress
● Responsibility for yourself	● Responsibility for yourself and possibly others
● You make the money	● You lose the money
● Freedom of working hours	● Working all the hours

"*The trouble is that good ideas are like gold dust – you have to sift through a lot of bad ideas before you come across your particular nugget.*"

Making a start

● Seven steps

From having a bright idea to actually making money from it seems a short enough route. But in reality it can be a lengthy trek rather than a short sprint. Making a start involves seven steps – which can take you a few weeks if you're lucky or a few years if you're not so lucky.

● Step 1: Thinking

Becoming self-employed is a big step for anyone. Having decided that you do want to change your work pattern, and that you do have the determination to succeed, think some more! Start by asking yourself some simple questions:

What?

What do you want to make or do? Is it a product or a service? Be clear in your mind what you are offering and don't feel tempted when friends suggest that you should also provide x, y and z. Stay with your original idea and keep it simple. Using the box on page 29, come up with a pithy statement of what you are trying to produce or the service you would like to provide. This, in business jargon, is a mission statement.

What are your skills? Why are you qualified to start the business? What are you good at doing? What areas of expertise and experience can you use to make the idea work?

Seven steps to becoming self-employed

1 Thinking
- What?
- How?
- Why?
- Where?
- Who?
- When?

2 Questioning
- Yourself
- Potential customers
- Family
- Friends

3 What's the big idea?
- New or old
- Quality or quantity

4 Testing
- Does it work?
- Market research
- Learning about the market

5 Timing
- Now
- Later
- Getting the time right

6 Creating
- Sole trader
- In partnership
- Franchise
- Limited company

7 Starting
- The first sale

What new skills do you need? Obviously running your own business demands different skills from working for an organisation. You have to honestly identify areas where you need to improve your skills. It may be you need to go on a computer course or that you need to learn business French – or both – but you have to identify any gaps in your knowledge and then attempt to fill them.

What skills? The following are just a small number of the skills you might already have, will need or would like to have. Some or all might be beneficial to your business. Use these as a starting point to answer the questions which follow.

What do you want to make or do

eg I want to use my experience in corporate catering to manage catering services for large companies based in the north-west.

- Man-management
- Basic accounting
- Computing
- Typing
- Languages
- Communication skills
- HGV licence
- Leadership skills

Skills you have	Skills you need	Skills you would like to have
1		
2		
3		
4		
5		

- Motivating others
- Self-motivation
- Selling skills
- Telephone skills
- Marketing skills
- Teamworking skills
- Working alone
- Written communication

How?

How will you make the product or provide the service?
Think of the basic process of making the product – will it need a lot of space or a lot of people? If it is a service, think of how you will provide it quickly, on time and to a high quality.

How will you make the product or provide the service?

Will it involve

☐ Just you

☐ You and one or two others

☐ A small number of full-time staff

☐ A large number of staff

☐ Occasional part-time workers

☐ A large amount of machinery and equipment

☐ Minimal machinery and equipment

How do you know it is something which people want?
Can you put it down to:

- **Experience**   While your experience may have convinced you of a business idea, tread carefully. Is your experience recent or appropriate? Was it formed in a different context? You still have to check that your conclusions are valid.

- **Intuition**   Many business people profess to having an innate understanding of what it is that people want. Politicians are also prone to speaking on behalf of the British people, without consulting more than a handful of like-minded individuals on a particular issue. If you are starting a business, you must back your beliefs with hard evidence.

- **Advice and opinions of others**   You should take the protestations of other people that something is a great idea with a pinch of salt. If something is a sure winner, you have to ask why aren't they doing it themselves? Invariably they will retort with an implausible excuse – too little time, too little money, etc.

- **Research**   To find out what people really think and the likelihood of them buying your product or service requires research.

Why?

Why do you think the business is a good idea? In the box opposite, write down another short explanation of why you think you and your business idea are viable. Think of why people will buy *your* particular product or service? Is it a truly new concept? Is it cheaper than the competition, easier to use or simply better quality?

Where?

It is early in the process, but still worth thinking about where you are going to do the work. If you want to open a greengrocer's shop the 'where' seems obvious enough – but you have to carefully consider the precise location which will best suit the business. This applies to all businesses. If you want to open a small manufacturing unit, you need to think of the optimal size and location – you will have to consider things like the size of the machines, the space taken by raw materials and stock, and the room needed for deliveries to be made.

Why do you think the business is a good idea?

eg Because I can supply a reliable, value-for-money, flexible, nourishing and tasty service on time, every time.

Where will you carry out the work?

Location

- ❑ An office
- ❑ A shop
- ❑ A factory
- ❑ A workshop
- ❑ At home

Who?

Who will buy it? This is the basic question which every business has to focus on – whether it is a giant multinational conglomerate or a corner shop. Without customers there will be no business. Anyone starting a business must have a clear idea of who the potential customers are and where they are.

Do you already know potential customers? If you are confident that there are customers out there, you may already know some. This can be vital as you develop your ideas.

Who will be involved in the business? Think of how many people will have to be involved in the business from the outset. These might include family, friends, your bank manager, your acccountant, full-time and part-time workers, as well as yourself. The box on page 36 provides the space for you to jot down your thoughts.

When?

When do you plan to start? Timescales vary from business to business. It might be feasible to start within a few weeks or it might take months, perhaps years, to get the business off the ground. At the moment, what do you consider to be a realistic timescale?

There is no need to provide instant or comprehensive answers to all of these questions. There are bound to be blind spots or areas which remain very vague – at this stage at least. These questions are not easy, but they need to be answered before you start your business. If you ignore them you increase the risk of missing the mark entirely.

The customers

Are they organisations or individuals?

Who actually makes the purchasing decision?

When?

What are their criteria for making the decision?

How do you know what the customers want?

Does the customer know what he or she wants?

Who will it be necessary to involve?		
Person	Status	What skills do they offer?
Accountant	Adviser	Financial advice; accounts; credit control

● Step 2: Questioning

It is always worth taking free advice and the richest source of advice and opinions may well be very close. Ask your family about your idea and how they think you are suited to being self-employed. Ask the people you work with, or those you worked with in the past. Ask friends and old contacts. Most importantly, ask questions of yourself. Think about what you are good at and where you need to develop your skills. Make a list. Accept any criticism as constructive. It is better to know your weaknesses – at least then you can begin to rectify them.

List the people whose advice you might find useful:

- Yourself
- Business contacts
- Family
- Friends
- Colleagues
- Former colleagues

● Step 3: What's the big idea?

Derek Wadlow runs a company called Motivity. He defines what the company does: 'By definition all our jobs are boring. Anything people don't want to do is grist for our mill.' In fact, Motivity has a turnover of over £750,000. Its business is difficult to describe but has, at one time or another, involved getting two tons of sand into one ounce bags for a board game; providing 500 artificial corpses at short notice for a horror film; and drilling two holes in several hundred eggs. No matter what the mundane task, Motivity is prepared to do it ... and make money from it. Such business brilliance may appear inspirationally simple. But it is not. In fact, Derek Wadlow decided to start his own business in 1967. 'I spent five years studying what sort of company I could create that required no capital, gave no credit, satisfied a demand, and had no competition.' In doing what other people can't or won't do, he created the business he imagined.

There are many people like Derek Wadlow who have worked hard at an idea and taken time to ensure it is a solid business proposition. This goes against the conventional wisdom that it only takes one great idea to make a fortune. The truth is that inspiration is only part of the battle; hard work and good fortune usually comprise the rest.

Entrepreneur Neil Howe, for example, took the longer route to starting his business, Packaging Interface, in 1990. 'I would wake up in the middle of the night and scribble ideas down,' he recalls. 'I kept thinking of better ways of doing it. In the end it took years to work everything all out.' For Neil the concern was not only the prospect of leaving the security of being an employee, but of fully understanding how his fledgling ideas would fit into the complex and organisationally rigid packaging industry.

Author and consultant Eddie Obeng launched Pentacle – The Virtual Business School in 1994. 'It took about two years from first having the idea,' he recalls. 'I spent time trying to figure out how I could achieve it with limited financial backing. As I was thinking, I floated the idea round colleagues and clients to see what they thought. I told them the concept to see what their reactions were. It is a matter of trying to get people involved. Unless they can see it and touch it they often won't do anything.'

In similar vein, management guru Edward de Bono observes: 'Everyone is surrounded by opportunities. But they only exist once they have been seen. And they will only be seen if they are looked for.'

The newspapers are full of advertisements offering 'superb' business opportunities. Take a selection from a single day:

Thyme to start your own spice and herb business.... No cold calling.... Minimum investment only £1,000	Turn what you earn in a month into what you earn in a week for as little as £13 plus effort
Start your own import/export agency. No capital, premises or experience required. No risk	**You'll have the fastest selling product of the decade. More than 90% of the people you talk to will buy the product on sight!**

Such propositions can fairly speedily be dismissed (especially ones that boast 'No risk'). But, having done so, you still have to find an opportunity of your own.

How do we identify an opportunity? It may appear to be ridiculously simple or simply ridiculous – a miraculous gadget which halves the amount of time taken by a household chore; a cunning attachment which reduces a car's fuel consumption. It doesn't really matter how stupid an idea for a product or service sounds. The question is whether people would be prepared to buy it.

Good ideas can strike at any time. In 1950, Frank McNamara was dining in a Manhattan restaurant. When the bill arrived he realised he had no cash. McNamara rang his wife to get him out of the embarrassing situation and began thinking how he could solve the problem. Within a few months he had persuaded 27 restaurants to join a credit card scheme under the name Diner's Club. Within a year the billings exceeded $1 million; the credit card was born.

Others take lessons from nature. After a day's hunting and with many burrs stuck to his clothes, Swiss engineer Georges de Mistral developed the idea of Velcro – a way of fastening fabrics firmly while leaving them easy to unfasten.

Sometimes ideas simply develop. Jean Widetch was trying to lose weight. She encouraged six of her friends to meet in her New York apartment to encourage each other. This was the birth of Weight Watchers – now in 24 countries and acquired by Heinz in 1978.

The golden rule was summed up by Aristotle Onassis: 'The secret of business is to know something that nobody else knows.' If the idea which no-one else knows happens to be a reflector placed in the middle of the road to help night-time visibility for drivers, the rewards are enormous. The idea does not have to be strikingly original. It can be distinctly unexciting. But it takes a particular – some would say wayward – mental approach to believe the mundane can be marvellous.

What's the big idea?

Is your idea

☐ original?

☐ an adaptation of another idea?

☐ a copy of an existing idea?

How is it different?

Why does it need to be different?

What makes a good idea?

Start with these four broad categories:

- Spot a need and come up with an inspired solution – such as cat's eyes, Velcro or Post-it notes

- Invent something, such as a game, which is tactile, challenging and ready for immediate use

- Take a popular product and improve or alter it – such as transforming roller skates into skateboards

- Change a traditional service or way of operating to make it more attractive or cheaper, or improve upon it by making it faster, more accurate, more trustworthy or of better quality.

> **"Research suggests that, on average, 60 ideas are needed before a single innovation is put into practice."**

The trouble is that good ideas are like gold dust – you have to sift through a lot of bad ideas before you come across your particular nugget. Research suggests that, on average, 60 ideas are needed before a single innovation is put into practice. A plethora of ideas is needed before one can be identified as deserving of implementation.

Remember, it doesn't have to be a new idea.

Few things are truly new. Genuine innovations are few and far between. You might come up with a genuinely new gadget or invention, but it is unlikely. In most fields large corporations are investing huge amounts of money in trying to come up with bright ideas. Anyone who can beat them to the solution deserves to make a million.

So, if a revolutionary new idea is unlikely (but not impossible), you are left with ideas which are new to you – this applies to a company going into a new field or adding a product to its portfolio; or improved old ideas – an enhanced version of an existing product or service which is repackaged, recycled or repositioned.

Further information

Protecting your idea might require a patent. For further information contact:

Patent Office & The Trademarks Registry
25 Southampton Buildings, Chancery Lane, London WC2A 1AW
Telephone: 0171-438 4700

The Chartered Institute of Patent Agents
Staple Inn Buildings, High Holborn, London WC1V 7PZ
Telephone: 0171-405 9450

> **Ways to improve an old product**
> 1 Change the colour
> 2 Add something new
> 3 Make it smaller
> 4 Make it bigger
> 5 Make it quicker
> 6 Use it for something new
> 7 Make it cheaper
> 8 Make it more expensive
> 9 Package it with something else
> 10 Improve service to customers
> 11 Sell it to new markets
> 12 Reduce its uses (make it specialist)
> 13 Expand its uses
> 14 Rename it

Think differently

It is amazing how many business success stories are built on doing routine things differently or making ordinary products differently. McDonald's is successful across the world, but there is nothing particularly original or innovative about what it does. You don't have to be one of the Le Roux brothers to serve up a tasty cheeseburger. Instead McDonald's does the simple things well. Its restaurants are clean; the food is consistent; the service is good. When McDonald's began its inspiration, Ray Kroc decided that these elements would differentiate McDonald's from all the other burger chains. 'It requires a certain kind of mind to see beauty in a hamburger bun,' reflected Kroc. He was right – no-one else manages to do the simple things as well.

The mistake many companies make is to continue thinking along traditional lines. SMH, the company marketing the 'Swatch' range of products, has achieved remarkable success by applying creative marketing principles. While other Swiss watchmakers went bust, Swatch learned lessons from other businesses. It made colourful and cheap watches which became fashion accessories. If it had simply tried to copy what others in the same business did it would have probably vanished into the corporate graveyard. In 1993, around 18 million Swatch watches were produced and the company launches up to 150 designs each year. It has become more than a disposable fashion item – Swatch products have been sold at auctions for £20,000 and there is an international club of collectors with 100,000 members. Swatch continues to do things differently. When it launched its 'Chandelier' model UK sales were restricted to 1,000. The company hired a shop in Covent Garden and sold the 1,000 watches by 4 pm – people travelled from Europe, the United States and the Far East for the launch.

'As a consequence of Swatch being one of the biggest brands in the world, it tends to be a serious business. That in itself is dangerous because the product is fun. We remind ourselves of that on a daily basis to ensure that the marketing does not lose the spontaneity and flexibility', says John Haynes, divisional director of Swatch UK.[1]

Creative approaches require that people learn to cast their attention and observing skills beyond the myopic perimeter of their own industry. Simply emulating each other in the same sector is a formula for incestuous stagnation. It often amounts to no more than doing the wrong things better and better. Looking elsewhere – even in the most unlikely places – can reinvent your entire approach.

Severn-Lamb makes steam locomotives. We all know that steam trains are a relic of the past but what Severn-Lamb has done is to discover new markets for an old product. Its turnover has risen from £1 million in 1989 to £4.5 million. The new market discovered by the company is leisure and theme parks – its customers include Europe's newest theme park, Port Aventura in Spain, Eurodisney and Entertainment City in Kuwait. In total 95 per cent of its production is exported. The philosophy of managing director Heinz Roosen is simply: 'If we don't take care of the customer, someone else will.'[2]

Learning from others has now acquired a label, 'benchmarking'. Benchmarking works on the principle that no matter what your business you can learn many lessons from the best in the business or from others in completely different fields.

---

[1] Quoted in H. Wayland, 'Marketing time', *Address*, Spring, 1994
[2] C. Arnot, 'Steaming on the right track', *Independent on Sunday*, 25 September, 1994

Helping you think differently

> **"Creative ideas can be wild, outlandish and impractical. On the other hand innovations must be practical, realistic and results-orientated."**
> Simon Majaro

'Creative ideas can be wild, outlandish and impractical. On the other hand innovations must be practical, realistic and results-orientated,' says Simon Majaro, author of *The Creative Gap*. 'Why bother with crazy ideas? The answer is simple. Many of the most successful innovations in the annals of business history started life as "intermediate impossibles". These are ideas which at first glance do not deserve a second look. Yet through a generous and imaginative analysis managed to be converted into implementable solutions.'

Simon Majaro identifies a number of approaches to enable companies to nurture and benefit from creative ideas.

Attribute listing is especially helpful in finding ways to improve an existing product or service. You list the current features or attributes of the firm's existing product and explore ways in which each one could be improved. A bank, for example, could list all the attributes its current services contain and then explore how each one of these attributes can be modified, improved and/or enriched. Provided such steps are taken in conjunction with a clear understanding of what the customers are looking for, the outcome can provide a creative platform for the development of customer-focused competitive advantage.

Brainstorming is a useful technique if managed effectively and carried out by someone with experience. Most people have had experience of brainstorming in the context of solving operational problems or exploring opportunities in day-to-day activities. But brainstorming can be applied to many other apparently imponderable problems and issues from finding a name for your company to developing strategy.

A variation on this theme is **pictorial brainstorming**. It is especially useful when the design of a new product concept is involved. For instance, if invited to add value to a 'Walkman' one can do it in a pictorial way and produce great ideas during the exercise. Participants are given a card and are asked to brainstorm pictorial images of a novel product or packaging. Every five minutes or so the card is passed on to the neighbour on the right who is invited to add some extra features or benefits to the drawing. After about six or seven such moves the results are explored in a plenary session and the various novel ideas explored.

Morphological analysis is an impressive name for a fairly simple method. Essentially it is a multi-dimensional matrix. Up to three dimensions can be shown graphically. If the number of dimensions exceeds three it can only be shown in columns of items where all the various permutations can be then listed, and if necessary with the aid of a computer. The idea underlying this technique is to identify a number of dimensions that may have a significant relevance to the ultimate nature of the product or service that you want to develop.

Read on

Simon Majaro, *The Creative Gap*, McGraw-Hill, Maidenhead, 1987

Another simple but popular technique is called **Mind mapping.** Created by Tony Buzan, this is based on the simple idea that writing things down using different colours is preferable to using a single colour. 'You only have to look at libraries all over the world to see that our places of learning are nothing short of giant public bedrooms, one big yawn,' says Buzan. It sounds childish and simple, but Buzan believes that Mind mapping makes meetings more effective and helps people make decisions more effectively. All that is needed is lots of paper and coloured felt-tip pens. It is worth remembering that Einstein, da Vinci and Van Gogh were all first-rate doodlers.

How to get Mind mapping

1 Arm yourself with blank sheets of A3 or A4 sized paper and lots of coloured felt-tip pens.

2 Relax, getting into the right frame of mind for new, creative thought and suspend belief in your inability to draw.

3 Select your key word or image and write or draw it within a box in the centre of the page.

4 Branch off any ideas related to this central theme, including thoughts which might seem obscure or irrational – they'll give you a fresh perspective on your subject.

5 Use one colour per branch with sub-branches flowing off from the centre, continuing until you've exhausted all possible links.

6 Condense your thoughts to one word per line so your mind is free to make a greater number of connections.

7 Use images instead of words wherever possible and draw boxes around or otherwise highlight important information. The more imaginative and colourful the Mind map, the more you will remember what's on it.

8 When you've exhausted the subject, edit and regroup your notes on a fresh sheet in order to produce your final, master Mind map.

Further information

Buzan Centres
Suites 2/3, Cardigan House ,37 Waterloo Road, Winton, Bournemouth Dorset BH9 1BD
Telephone: 01202 533593

Beware the brilliant bad idea

There are many common signs which may point to an idea not being such a good business idea. These include:

- **The ego**   Some ideas are so persuasively wonderful, so obviously winners, that it is incredible that no-one else seems to think so. 'I am right. I know I am right,' say their originators with rising exasperation. If you are the only person in the world who thinks that something is a good idea, sooner or later you will have to question your own judgement.

- **The smart solution**   Plenty of good ideas solve problems which don't actually exist. If you invent an egg unscrambler which returns scrambled eggs to their original form you will appear on TV programmes, but you will not make a fortune.

- **The imaginary customer**   It is no good simply to imagine who the customers might be. You have to know exactly who will be buying the product, why, where and how much they are prepared to pay.

● Step 4: Testing

One evening in 1900, a group of people lay flat on their faces on the floor of a room in the house of British engineer Hubert Booth. With their handkerchiefs between their mouths and the floor, they proceeded to suck dust from the carpet and collect it on their handkerchiefs. This, absurd as it seems, was part of the development of Booth's great idea, now indispensable in any modern household. It was patented in 1901 as the vacuum cleaner.

Every idea has to work. This may seem glaringly obvious, but many businesses fail to take off simply because not enough time has been spent discovering whether the product works and whether it works reliably enough to satisfy customers. If something works perfectly efficiently once or twice and then self-destructs, you are likely to have a lot of dissatisfied customers knocking on your door fairly soon. The product or service must work, but remember that it also has to be flexible. You can't simply say this is the product; this is what it does; do you want to buy it? At the testing stage it is worth considering how the product can be customised or made more flexible. Think of other situations in which it could be used, or other people who might benefit from using it.

Flexibility is a key competitive weapon for the small business. Small firms can compete successfully with large organisations, because they can absorb fluctuations in demand through their flexibility. They can be innovative in coming up with customised and quality products or services; flexibly targeting niches in local markets, or at the higher end of the market; and in providing better service to customers with special contractual relationships and strong feelings of loyalty. This sort of flexibility needs to be built into the product or service from the very start of your enterprise.

Who can you test your product on?

Potential customers

Colleagues

Friends

Family

Other contacts

Testing of potential customers or users requires that your idea is fairly well developed. In this sort of test the key factors are:

- ***approach the right people*** – are they really potential purchasers?

- ***provide an incentive*** – such as an opportunity to make the first purchase at a discounted price.

- ***seek more general information*** – don't restrict questions to your own business, ask their opinion of competing products, prices, services, etc.

- ***meet face-to-face*** – you are more likely to extract a large amount of information if you meet face-to-face.

- ***make it as realistic as possible*** – it is no use asking questions which are vague and theoretical. 'Would you be interested in buying this?' is an important question but needs to be backed up:
  - at what price?
  - at what time?
  - in what form?
  - should it be changed? And, if so, in what way?
  - how should we approach you?

- ***learn lessons and implement them*** – it is important to talk, listen and act.

Learning about the market

You should gather as much information as possible about customers, the market and competitors. There are many possible sources of information:

- reference libraries
- trade exhibitions and conferences
- trade publications and magazines

- trade organisations and associations
- market analysis and data.

Read on

Croner's Reference Book for the Self-Employed and Smaller Business, Croner Publications, Kingston, Telephone: 0181-547 3333

If you are opening a shop you can receive free copies of the trade magazines *Independent Grocer* and *Convenience Store*. You need to find out if there is a trade publication relevant to your business. If so, you might be able to receive free copies or, if it is useful, you could subscribe to it.

Knowing your competitors

Think of your competitors – and other companies whose approach you admire. They may not seem directly applicable to what you do, but identify the company and think whether its approaches could be used in your business. Pinpointing areas which you believe are important in your business is useful in itself. If there are competitors or other companies which have particular lessons for your business try and find out more about their particular approach.

Which company do you think:	Are its approaches applicable to your business?
● produces quality products?	
● has consistent, quality service?	
● offers value for money products?	
● uses the latest technology successfully?	
● has advanced production facilities?	
● has the most reliable delivery systems?	
● has the best marketing?	
● has the best management?	
● has the best working practices?	

● Step 5: Timing

Having reassured yourself that your idea is still a good idea which works, the next step is to determine whether the world is ready to buy it. In the business world timing is everything.

> **"In the business world timing is everything"**

Some ideas are merely launched at the wrong time. Some ideas are ahead of their time. The *European* newspaper, for example, is an idea which might yet prove a success. Some ideas are behind their time. CB Designs provides aluminium and stone signs for golf courses. The company was set up by chartered accountant Chris Boxall. 'We think we have got the product right, but what has gone wrong is the time it has taken to get everything organised and the fact that it was a terrible time to set up such a business,' he observed as the business was becoming established.

There is, of course, some degree of luck involved. You can't be held accountable for acts of God or politicians. But you can for virtually any other event, so there are a number of factors worth considering:

- *Is the product or service subject to seasonal variations in demand? If so, how can you reduce these variations or organise the business so that they are not financially disastrous?*
- *When would be the best time for the launch?*
- *Are the people who make the purchasing decision working on a budget cycle?* Companies invariably have budgets which are allocated at certain times of the year – you need to find out when your potential customer has the money at their disposal.
- *When will you receive the maximum publicity?*

It is worth remembering at this point that even the most brilliant ideas can initially be rejected or dismissed. The inventor of the copier machine, Chester Carlson, had his idea rejected by 20 companies. And though he patented the idea in 1937, it was not until 1959 that a workable office copier came into being. Many other good ideas had similarly inauspicious beginnings. Richard Drew invented masking tape and 'Scotch Cellulose Tape'. Launched in 1930, Scotch Tape totalled $33 in its first year of sales.

These ideas were good ones and they worked, the trouble was that in the case of the copier the product needed a lot more work and, in the case of Scotch Tape, people were unaware of the full range of its possible uses. Sir Clive Sinclair has commented: 'I invent things when I perceive people's need – it is then a matter of convincing people they need it.' Convincing people can take a long time – and a great deal of money. It is preferable if they are aware of the need and you appear to answer it.

Timing it right

Think of the events and activities in the year which will affect your business. If you are going to make garden sheds, for example, you are probably likely to sell more during the spring when people tend to tidy up their gardens and prepare them for the summer.

Month	Plus points	Minus points
January		
February		
March		
April		
May		
June		
July		
August		
September		
October		
November		
December		

● Step 6: Creating

What kind of business will it be?

Sole trader

The most straightforward form of business is being a sole trader. Becoming a sole trader involves few complications – you don't have to become a limited company, but you do have to tell your Tax Office and the Department of Social Security that you are now self-employed. Being a sole trader suits many forms of business. If you are working for yourself as a window cleaner, a decorator, writer, gardener or plumber, with a simple business not involving huge financial investments or large numbers of staff it is ideal. The downside is that you are personally liable for any debts.

Partnership

Partnerships can prove difficult. You have to be sure that your business partner is someone you can work with. The parameters as to how you work need to be clear from the outset. As partners you are both accountable for the business's debts, contracts and tax payments. The reasons for going into partnership may include:

- ● *complementary skills* – one person may be a specialist, the other a generalist, and they both feel the need for the other's support and expertise. For example, one partner may be good at selling, the other at administration.

- ● *wanting to share the burden* – it can appear that a business halved is a business with half the worries and responsibilities. This is unlikely to be the case.

- ● *damage limitation* – you want your partner's knowledge and expertise on your side rather than as a competitor.

Only the first reason is practically viable. A partnership has to be made to work like any other relationship. If you enter into it for negative reasons or with misgivings it is likely to quickly encounter problems. You need, therefore, to map out a partnership agreement with a solicitor (if you don't you are ruled by the antique legislation of the 1890 Partnership Act). Among the issues your agreement might consider are:

- What your different roles and jobs will be. Dividing jobs up at the start might prevent argument later.
- How the partnership's profits are going to be divided and how much income each of the partners will earn.
- A clause preventing either partner setting up in competition with the other.
- The value of each partner's share.
- How arguments should be settled.

The agreement must cover as many eventualities as can be imagined and can include matters as diverse as who can sign the partnership's cheques to what happens if one of the partners dies.

Limited Company

While sole traders and partners have unlimited liability establishing a limited company, as its name suggests, provides limited liability. Your house and possessions are no longer under threat. The most that shareholders can lose is what they have already invested in the company. For many, limited company status confers a degree of respectability and seriousness. There is no doubt that investors, for example, take a limited company more seriously. On the surface at least, being a limited company sounds more professional. But as you can buy a limited company for a few hundred pounds, this is a mistaken belief.

To make it worthwhile you need to be a significant business with substantial assets and turnover. It does cost money – you have to employ auditors to check your accounts, file returns to Companies House, pay corporation tax and not forgetting the sign you need outside the premises to inform people who you are. You may also become an employee paying income tax and national insurance through PAYE.

A limited company has a minimum of two members and a secretary. It is a legal entity rather than a person and gives you the protection of not being personally liable for the company's debts. But you have to be wary of carrying on running the business when it is technically insolvent – when it owes more than its assets. If you do so you can become personally liable.

Further information

Companies Registration Office
Companies House, Crown Way, Maindy, Cardiff CF4 3UZ
Telephone: 01222 388588

Franchising

It is extremely difficult and demanding to come up with an original business idea that will work. One way round this is to become a franchisee. Franchising takes a business idea that works and gives you the opportunity to try and make it work in your particular area. The principle is simple: the franchisor has the idea and an already existing business. You then become a franchisee, probably pay for the costs of setting up the new business, agree to pay a certain amount of the business' revenue, and then set up the business following the formula or suggestions of the franchisor.

Franchising began nearly 50 years ago in the United States. It is now a huge business. In total there are estimated to be 25,000 franchise outlets in the United Kingdom under around 400 different franchise companies. Their annual turnover is estimated at around £5 billion.

Franchising can cover a huge range of activities. In the 1990s 8,000 franchised milk delivery rounds have been set up in the United Kingdom. There are many other opportunities – restaurant chains, printing (Prontaprint), cleaning services (such as Service Master), sandwich shops (Prêt a Manger in London now sells franchises). McDonald's, Kentucky Fried Chicken, Tie Rack, Burger King and Holiday Inn are some of the household names run as franchises. Holiday Inn has mushroomed over the last 20 years to 1,500 hotels.

The advantages of running a franchise are many:

- It can allow your business to be instantly **national** in its coverage. If there are franchises throughout the country you are, in effect, part of a national organisation with all the benefits this brings – other franchises may put business your way; the name of the company or brand may be well known.

- It also supplies instant **competitive advantage**. You will probably be given exclusive rights to use the product or service in a particular area.

- **Back-up**. The nightmare for the small business man or woman is not knowing something and having no-one to turn to (unless they pay for professional advice). A franchise offers important back-up with, for example, marketing and training support. A national company also brings with it the advantages of bulk buying. In theory at least, the support you receive should enable you to avoid common pitfalls such as renting the wrong or inappropriate premises.

It is not an easy route to instant success. 'Franchising is not the easiest way of running a business,' observes Brian Smart of the British Franchising Association. So, what can go wrong?

Who knows best?

Some franchises have floundered when the franchise company and the franchisee have fallen out or simply failed to agree on how the business should be run. The health food chain, Holland & Barrett, began selling franchises in the 1980s, but put a halt to the process after experiencing trouble in managing the franchises. The trouble comes when the thorny question of who actually runs the business is not clear. While the franchise company believes it has a winning formula, the franchisee will want to do things his or her way. If a balance isn't struck the business is likely to satisfy neither side.

Poor monitoring

Franchises require a formula to be effectively shared. If the franchisor does not monitor the performance of the franchisee, there is the danger that the franchisor will make mistakes which have already been made elsewhere or head up a succession of blind alleys.

Weak brand

The stronger the brand, the more likely is success. If the franchise is built on a weak or not commonly known brand, the chances of success are reduced.

Clearly, selecting the right franchise is crucial:

- Take your time and talk to a number of possible companies

- Select one that has a track record of franchise success. The best companies have slowly and carefully built their franchise operations. Beware of those which suddenly appear with a good idea and are trying to establish 50 franchises around the country virtually overnight. The attraction of a franchise is that you are backing an established winner – if the company is only a winner in a single location it may not fare so well elsewhere.

To find out more it is worth attending the many franchise exhibitions and conferences which are held regularly throughout the country. There is a British Franchise Association which has a helpline and there are magazines on franchising.

Further information

British Franchising Association
Franchise Chamber, Thames View, Newtown Road, Henley-on-Thames RG9 1HG
Telephone: 01491 578049

● Stage 7: Starting

If you have carried out the six previous steps you should be ready to start your business.

Who can help?

Not so long ago, the answer to this question would have been an abrupt no-one. Now there are a plethora of organisations which are there to help people start their own business and run it successfully. Many are run and funded by the government. Among the organisations which specialise in small business advice are:

● The Department of Employment runs a Small Firms Service which can be contacted free on 0800 222999

● The Department of Trade and Industry has a huge number of initiatives and various forms of funding. These change regularly so it is difficult to keep track of what is on offer, to who and where. For the latest information it is advisable to contact your local DTI office:

General enquiries for DTI: 0171–215 5000
DTI North East: 0191–232 4722
DTI North West (Manchester): 0161–838 5000
DTI North West (Liverpool): 0151–224 6300
DTI Yorkshire & Humberside: 01532–443171
DTI East Midlands: 01602–506181
DTI West Midlands: 0121–212 5000
DTI East: 01223–461939
DTI South East (London): 0171–215 0572
DTI South East (Reading): 01734–395600
DTI South East (Reigate): 01737–226900
DTI South West: 01272–272666
The Scottish Office Industry Department: 0141–248 4774
Welsh Office Industry Department: 01222–823185

Department for Economic Development for Northern Ireland: 01232–763244

Business Links

A network of Business Links are now being developed round the United Kingdom to provide high quality business support services through a single local access point. Each Business Link is a partnership of local providers of business support services, including Training and Enterprise Councils (TECs), Chambers of Commerce, Local Authority and Enterprise Agencies. Through Business Link businesses will be able to get advice and information on all aspects of developing their business, a diagnostic service or business health check, counselling and specialist consultancy help, and teams of personal business advisers, specially trained to provide ongoing support. With 50 already open, the long-term aim is a national network of 200 local centres.

Further information on Business Links can be obtained from your local Government Regional Office, TEC or by calling 01742 597507

Banks

Always anxious to attract small business accounts, many banks provide information on setting up your own business. NatWest, for example, published an excellent guide on starting up a business and *Making the most of your business* for businesses that are already established. Further information on what banks have to offer can be obtained from local branches.

The Forum of Private Business

Founded in 1977, FPB is a non-profit, non-partisan organisation with a national membership of 21,000 private business owners. Its principal aim is to ensure that private business owners have a voice in the legislation and other issues which affect the profitability of their businesses. It runs a number of high profile campaigns, such as on prompt payment to small businesses.

The Forum of Private Business
Ruskin Chambers, Drury Lane, Knutsford, Cheshire WA16 6HA
Telephone: 01565–634467

National Association of Shopkeepers and Self-Employed

Formed in 1942 to protect and enhance the interests of the independent shopkeeper, this organisation has now extended to include all self-employed people. It provides help in a number of areas including dealing with VAT decisions and penalties, employment disputes, rent and leases, and Inland Revenue investigations.

National Association of Shopkeepers and Self-Employed
Lynch House, 91 Mansfield Road, Nottingham NG1 3FN
Telephone: 01602 475046

Association of Independent Businesses
133 Copeland Road, London SE15 3SP
Telephone: 0171-277 5158

Alliance of Small Firms and Self-Employed People
33 The Green, Clane, Wilts SN11 8DJ
Telephone: 01249 817003

Institute of Independent British Business
12 Orange Street, London WC2H 7ED
Telephone: 0171-839 1233

Institute of Small Business
14 Willow Street, London EC2A 4BH
Telephone: 0171-638 4937

National Federation of Self-Employed and Small Businesses
32 St Anne's Road West, Lytham St Annes, Lancs FY8 1NY
Telephone: 01253 720911

● Planning your start

You can now draft a rough plan of how and when you are going to accomplish these seven stages. You need to be flexible. Strict schedules may motivate you, but there is no point rushing forward if your market research reveals fundamental flaws in your product or complete apathy in the marketplace.

The stages do not have to be completed or contemplated in isolation. After the thinking stage, many stages can be under way at the same time.

Action	Date	Who	Date Completed by
Thinking			
Questioning			
The big idea			
Testing			
Timing			
Creating			
Starting			

> *Most people in business have little idea of just how many different skills they have to possess to make a living.*
>
> *In any one day, often in any one hour, they have to assume the role of product specialist, salesman or woman, motivator, accountant, public speaker, mentor, coach and many more.*

What skills do you need?

Running a business involves a huge variety of skills. Indeed, the Forum of Private Business estimates that a business owner makes decisions on over 3,000 issues in any one year. The sheer number of issues which those in business have to deal with and the skills required can easily be under estimated. Most people in business have little idea of just how many different skills they possess to make a living. In any one day, often in any one hour, they have to assume the role of product specialist, salesman or woman, motivator, accountant, public speaker, mentor, coach and many more.

Just think of the skills you use in a day's work. Which of the following skills do you think you use regularly?

- ❏ decision-making
- ❏ project management
- ❏ written communication
- ❏ making presentations
- ❏ accounting and book-keeping
- ❏ foreign languages
- ❏ negotiating
- ❏ word processing
- ❏ computer skills
- ❏ selling
- ❏ marketing
- ❏ coaching

- communicating with employees
- communicating with customers
- communicating with suppliers
- communicating with the media
- communicating with shareholders
- delegating
- motivating
- persuading
- managing meetings
- condensing information.

Now think which of these skills do you use every day and which do you rarely or never use?

There are two dangers lurking behind this pot-pourri of skills:

1 **The specialist** We have all met specialists. They are the small business equivalent of anoraks. They have a bright idea and know everything there is to know about it. If they make something, they are more than willing to give you a blow-by-blow account of every aspect of the production process in intricate detail. They are specialists to a fault. While they may know the exact pressure their product could bear on top of Everest, they are unlikely to know how many they sold last month or the idea behind the latest promotional campaign. They are poor with figures and uninterested in marketing. Customers are an incidental detail (though some are okay because they appear quite interested in the thermodynamic qualities of the product).

2 **The generalist** At the opposite extreme are the generalists. They are handicapped by the fact that they are adequate at everything and exceptional at nothing. This appears an ideal situation for someone in a small business. After all, I have just pointed out how many skills you have to master. The trouble is that the terminal generalists tend to have to continually move swiftly. They are unable to sit down and really master details. Instead, they flit to the next activity. In

the end they do a great many jobs badly. They tend, therefore, to measure their effectiveness by how busy they are. To them, a 15-hour day is nothing. They have to put so many hours in simply because they rarely achieve anything concrete. If you question the wisdom of working such long hours they become defensive, but fail to make the time to consider how they could work more effectively or how 15-hour days affect your health and family.

It is important, therefore, to avoid extremes or to recognise which of these two extreme categories you are liable to fall into. If you are a specialist in a particular area, you will have to ensure that you employ other people to handle the parts of the business which you are simply not interested in and unable to carry out effectively. If you are a generalist you will have to exercise self-discipline and sit down to complete tasks.

You don't have to be a genius

It is a mistake to believe that success relies on either qualifications or huge reservoirs of intelligence. You don't have to be a genius to succeed. Indeed, geniuses have a poor track record when it comes to running businesses. A lack of formal qualifications need hold no-one back from business success. Lord Hanson, Sir Colin Marshall of BA, Lord Wolfson of Great Universal Stores, Brian Pitman, chief executive of Lloyds Bank, Sir William Purves, head of the Hong Kong and Shanghai Bank, are just some of the eminent business leaders who have risen to the top unhindered by university degrees.

> **"You don't have to be a genius to succeed."**

While formal qualifications are not necessary, research is constantly unveiling the exact ingredients which make for successful business people. 'You cannot be successful at anything doing it for 90 per cent of the time,' Arne Naess, Norwegian shipowner, has observed. Research repeatedly suggests that those people who succeed have:

- ***drive and energy*** – they soak up work as surely as sponges soak up water

- **broad experience** – they have worked in a variety of different organisations, doing different jobs

- **international exposure** – many have worked abroad or have other international experience

- **time management** – they are adept at prioritising what needs to be done and by who.

'You have to be very disciplined. You have to make sure you don't waste any time. Use every hour,' says Trevor Hemmings who has succeeded in a variety of business ventures – including buying Pontins Holiday camps and then selling them to Scottish & Newcastle. 'Nobody personally does anything, unless you sail a yacht round the ocean. But if you think about the problems all night, you come into work next morning and you know what you're going to do, and you have an advantage. That's why you're the boss.'[1]

It is impressive that some business people manage to survive on four hours' sleep and read strategic reports at 3 am. But at 3 am the average chief executive is sound asleep. Generally they are not superman or superwoman. They just work extremely hard and, more importantly, they work effectively.

You don't have to be a specialist

Frank Hornby invented Meccano. He wasn't an engineer or a mechanic, but making toys was a hobby. Patented in 1901, by 1914 Meccano was established across the world and continues to thrive. You don't have to be a specialist. Indeed, you may know very little about the technical side of your business. A greengrocer does not need to know the methods of production employed to produce the oranges sold in his or her shop. In the same way as great sports coaches are not necessarily great athletes, the business owner doesn't have to know everything. Indeed, a desire to know everything can be dangerous.

---

[1] Quoted in the *Independent on Sunday*, 20th November 1994

The chief executives of major companies are not there because of their specialist product knowledge. The head of IBM is not a computer programmer; the head of BP is not a geologist or a chemical engineer. They are experts at business (not necessarily their own business). Identifying the major skills needed by the self-employed is practically impossible. A market trader needs to have different skills to those of a landscape gardener. But key elements may be common to both. These might include:

- Intuition
- Decision-making
- Communication
- Selling
- Marketing
- Negotiating
- Sweat and obsession.

● Intuition

There is a stereotypical image of the entrepreneur who makes good. They are inspirational and charismatic, persuasive and colourful. Entrepreneurs are exciting; business men or women are frequently dull. (This is something worth remembering when you talk to your bank manager who may have a preference for the latter.) They charm people and it is hard to imagine them failing. They have the Midas touch. Richard Branson falls into this category. It is tempting to try and emulate such people. Unfortunately, this is probably a waste of time. Wearing a colourful jumper and growing a beard does not give you Richard Branson's entrepreneurial instincts.

The best entrepreneurs seem to start early in life. Richard Branson did and Gary Withers, founder of the design and communication company Imagination, certainly did. The nine-year-old Gary Withers ran a syndicated blackberry picking company from his garage, giving children maps and boxes before despatching them to pick blackberries. By the age of 12 he was sewing wedding marquees on his mother's machine. In 1993 his company ran projects in 28 countries and was worth £30 million. Management guru Tom Peters labelled Imagination as 'a paradigm of the successful company for the next century'.

But don't be put off. There aren't many people like Gary Withers or Richard Branson. Self-employed people do not have to be zany and inspirational, though it certainly helps in many businesses. The trouble is that the skills you need in the first place, when coming up with and developing a good business idea, are not necessarily those you will need as the business grows. That is why some people specialise in starting up businesses and others concentrate on other aspects of management such as saving failing businesses.

Business history repeatedly proves that it is one thing to have a bright idea, quite another to run a business. 'I was borrowing money from 30 leading banks. How could they all be wrong? I'm only a simple businessman,' said Freddie Laker when asked why his company went bust. He believed the support of his banks was validation of his idea for a cheap transatlantic airline.

> **"The men in colourful jumpers are invariably backed by people in dull suits."**

'Entrepreneurs should not be involved in running businesses,' says Sir Clive Sinclair. They have a tendency to be blinded by their own inventiveness, believing that if there is a problem inspiration will strike and the problem will disappear. The first word of caution, therefore, is not to be seduced by your own brilliance. Even the most inspired ideas require careful consideration and examination. The men in colourful jumpers are invariably backed by people in dull suits.

Even so, we all make important decisions based on an inexplicable feeling which to others may seem a whim. 'I am a rational man but the biggest decisions you take on instinct,' said Osvaldo Ardilles when he became manager of Tottenham Hotspur (his reaction to his dismissal was more rational – 'I did it my way'). Whether taking over a football team, buying a house or moving into a new business market, we all act on instinct, gut-feeling, hunch, intuition, call it what you will. In fact, all the data in the world is unlikely to change your mind if your intuition tells you something is a good idea. Unfortunately, intuition cannot be measured and is difficult to explain. Investors are unlikely to be impressed by a business plan based on a hunch. Shareholders would undoubtedly feel a little worried if the chief executive admitted that the strategy came to him while he was in the bath.

Although it is constantly at work, intuition has had a bad press. Managers distrust it and investors run away from it. But, for many people, intuition is a critical part of their job. Stock Exchange traders don't have time to call a meeting before they sell or buy; they back their intuition. Intuition is a vital element of staff selection. Recruitment consultants need to base their decisions on objective data. This is what they are paid for. But, in reality, people are invariably selected because of intuitive judgement. All the candidates can do the job, but for some reason the recruiter feels they can work better with X than with Y. It is personal chemistry and, to some extent, prejudice.

Making the wrong intuitive decision can prove extremely costly. According to some it is an area where women are better equipped than men. While women are comfortable admitting that someone is more suited to the job without having any hard facts and figures, men tend to come to hard and fast judgements.

Venture capitalist, Robert Drummond, former chairman of Grosvenor Venture Managers, agrees: 'Intuition is all about flexibility – being tuned into what's going on and being prepared to change direction.' By its very nature, venture capital relies on hunches about whether a business is likely to succeed or fail. According to Robert Drummond, it is not simply a question of backing winners. 'It is no good following rigid rules in business. Successful people not only make the right decisions, they have a grasp of timing. Being a venture capitalist is all about being opportunistic, using your intuition to identify changes in society and to invest in areas which meet new needs.'

Some argue that intuition comes with experience. 'Very senior managers often appear to operate intuitively,' says psychologist Robert Sharrock of Young, Samuel, Chambers (YSC). 'They don't use the usual buzz-words or adhere to textbook models of management. It is like mastering a skill or craft – putting it into practice becomes automatic. A lot of intuition is, in fact, highly skilled.'

Less experienced, younger managers are therefore unlikely to have the necessary intuitive skills to make instant decisions. 'For managers who have a lot of experience and intelligence, intuitive judgements are probably reliable. Others need to be extremely cautious,' says Robert Sharrock.

With increasing emphasis on the speed of decision-making, intuition is likely to increase in importance. 'Uncertainty breeds intuition,' says Professor Colin Carnall of Henley Management College. 'Things now happen so fast that managers rarely have all the information they might need to make a decision. They have to rely on their intuition if they are to seize the opportunity.'

Professor Carnall believes intuitive managers, willing to back their judgements with immediate action, are the people who get to the top. 'Senior managers are not necessarily the most intelligent. Usually they are pragmatic and flexible, able to make intuitive decisions quickly and reliably, rather than waiting for exhaustive analysis.'

Intuition teetered on the edge of respectability in the 1980s. The image of the dashing entrepreneur was in part based on a dislike of the stereotypically dull accountant-manager. Who needs flow charts when running businesses is intuitive? Intuition was all about mobile phones, deals and continually hustling. A decade later, reality is dawning and intuition is increasingly seen as a skill which can be learned.

'Intuition is the ability to learn from experience,' says Robert Drummond. 'Companies need intuitive people – not necessarily at the very top of the organisation.' Indeed, some organisations, such as 3M, have built their reputation on encouraging people throughout the company to follow their intuition.

Research carried out by Ashridge Management College's Phil Hodgson suggests that managers who use their intuition effectively and continuously are likely to have a number of clear characteristics:

- They make decisions quickly and confidently; they are willing to back their judgement and don't spend large periods of time weighing things up.
- They use data only when necessary – not for them the computer print-out containing every single statistic available.
- They recognise intuition as a skill, part of their managerial armoury.
- They accept and encourage ideas whatever their source or apparent usefulness, at every stage.
- They act on intuitive judgements, rather than questioning them.
- They accept no rigid or wrong method of doing things – if something feels, looks or seems right they will do it.

● Decision-making

Decision-making has never been more demanding – or more important – in business and in our personal lives. But all too often we find ourselves caught like rabbits in the glare of headlights, trapped by our own indecision. Though we make hundreds of decisions every day, we don't even remember making the vast majority. Nevertheless, bad decisions stick in our minds. 'Nothing is more difficult and therefore more precious than to be able to decide,' observed Napoleon. Though Napoleon realised that decision-making was critical, he still decided to go to Russia in the depths of winter. No doubt he pondered at length on the limitations of his own decision-making in later life.

History is cluttered with blunders on a colossal scale, whether they be military (such as the Charge of the Light Brigade) or managerial. The *Independent on Sunday* ran a series where business people admitted to the worst decision they ever made. And all their bad decisions were remembered with appalling clarity – the embarrassment, the financial loss, the meeting with the hysterical boss.

For anyone in business, decision-making is a vital part of the job. Indeed, one definition of management is deciding what to do and getting it done. So, no matter what the business, decision-making matters. A decision is a commitment to action. The importance of making the right decisions has led to the growth of a lucrative industry. There are many academics and consultants, and some charlatans, who earn their livings from instructing people on how they could make the right decisions every time.

Theories abound. There are a host of handy hints and techniques. There is, for example, something called a 'decision tree' which is used by people tortured by indecision. The tree charts all the possible outcomes of a number of different options as well as their likely outcomes. Each of the chain of events is then given a probability and monetary value. The manager, undaunted by the number of charts, is then expected to make a decision. The tree may be highly accurate, but hardly provides for speedy decisions.

There are other approaches. Social scientist Herbert Simon has been studying the decision-making process for many years. Using computers to simulate thought patterns, Simon has defined three steps towards making a decision. The first is intelligence, identifying a situation which calls for a decision. The second is design, conceiving and developing alternative courses of action and assessing their implications.

Finally, there is choice, selecting which of the alternatives to proceed with. The trouble with Simon's analysis is that humans are less reliable than machines. Given a neat process, they will insist on doing all three stages at once or missing one out altogether.

In the real world of compromise and incompetence, other thinkers have concluded that the decisions we reach are rarely the most rational. In fact, many are entirely irrational, reliant on hunches and instincts even we don't understand. Some managers appear to have built their entire careers on such decisions. In their book, if you have come up with complex calculations to justify a decision it's probably the wrong one in the first place. If you are in business you simply can't wait for information to determine everything. Instead, many blunder off down the most ill-advised route conceivable and sometimes happen upon the solution.

In the past, decision-making was regarded as an innate skill that you either had or didn't have. But, given practice and awareness, effective – or at least improved – decision-making can be learned. Untrained decision-makers make a number of common errors which prevent them from getting it right time after time. They are not earth-shattering. The fact is that we have all, at one time or another, made a bad decision than can be attributed to one of the traps.

- **Only fools rush in**   The first common error is plunging in, rushing and acting on the first idea that comes to mind. For business people intent on being people of action, it is a tempting option. People are impressed by the immediate decision. Responding quickly, they argue, is what running a business is all about. If it's the wrong course at least you find out fairly quickly and can set off down another route. The trouble is that decision-making by trial and error can be an expensive, not to say time-consuming, means of reaching the right decision.

- **Solving the wrong problem**   Linked to the first common error is setting out to solve the wrong problem because you have approached it with predetermined ideas. The history of business is littered with people who did not remove the blinkers. They carry on trying to solve the old problems while their eventual conquerors are looking at things differently and coming up with solutions appropriate to the times. In effect, they refuse to accept changes in circumstances. 'Heavier than air flying machines are impossible,' announced Lord Kelvin in 1895. While he was considering aeroplanes as impossible, others were inventing them.

- ***Being too inflexible*** If you define the problem too strictly you eliminate a wide range of possible solutions. Alternatively, you might be overly influenced by the views and prejudices of others you talk to. Listening to the views of others is valuable, but there's not much to be gained from blindly following someone else's ideas.

- ***Overconfidence*** We have to believe in our own judgement, yet we forget the many mistakes we have made, the decisions that have misfired. The truth is that we are not always right. Overconfidence has been ruthlessly punished in history – look at Pearl Harbor.

- ***The convenience route*** Using rules of thumb or the most conveniently available information to make a decision is a sure way of getting it wrong. This is part of an overall problem of not being systematic, not keeping track of the developing decisions.

The fashionable solution to some of these problems is to organise people into teams. The theory is that more brains make for better decisions, but, in practice, it is not always the case. Juries, for example, make mistakes. In a group of people there is an assumption that somewhere along the line someone will come up with the right decision. Even if you sit back at the relevant meetings and look into the distance, someone will be making copious notes and will guide everyone along to the right decision. This system makes everyone feel better. They can take the credit for good ideas, even though they were dozing steadily at the time, and distance themselves from the bad ones ('I fought them long and hard over that one, but they insisted it went in, now look what's happened').

Another potentially dangerous assumption is that experience automatically leads to learning and, therefore, better decision-making. Of course, experience is inevitable whether it is good, bad or indifferent. Simply going into work to do the same job in the same way year after year gives us an ability to make the right sort of decisions. At a simple level this is true. Some decisions are basic and automatic. But what if they are ever so slightly out of the ordinary? Experience may well be inevitable; the trouble is that learning is not. Someone might have had the same job for 30 years and still have only one year's experience 30 times. If you don't audit the effectiveness of your decisions, how are you to know if they have been successful or that you are a good decision-maker?

There are a host of lists suggesting how to become a good decision-maker. Few are foolproof, but most boil down to the following six stages to a perfect decision.

1 **What's your objective?** If you don't know what you want or what you need to solve, you are unlikely to make the best decision for your business.

2 **What's involved?** You need to consider the elements involved in the decision. Who will it affect and how?

3 **What are the possible solutions?** Canvass opinions and gather information so you know the full range of options which you can choose from. Don't discount any too early in your thinking and don't focus narrowly on what you think the solution should be.

4 **Make your decision** Plump for a particular option, having carefully weighed up the pros and cons.

5 **Present it to others** What do other people think of the decision. Check their feelings and misgivings. Do you still think you are right?

6 **Make it happen** Implement the decision.

It is all perfectly logical and, if you are caught in the relentless hurly burly of business life, probably totally impossible to implement. No-one could be that perfect! But when it comes to major decisions, you do need some sort of process to get it right. Otherwise you run the risk of decisions which not everyone supports and ones that are plain wrong.

● Communication

Communication is a vital skill. You will have to communicate effectively with a large number of people in a variety of ways. You may be passionate about your idea or business, but if you cannot communicate with your customers, your bank manager, your suppliers and your staff in a way they understand then you will find yourself with problems.

Be consistent

If you own or run the business what you say counts and is important to the people you deal with. It can reassure employees, placate customers and appease lenders. Alternatively, it can irritate, confuse and disillusion all of these parties. The key must be consistency. You must repeat important messages and reinforce them by your behaviour. It is little use berating someone for throwing away a paperclip, if you have just bought a helicopter for the use of senior managers only.

Avoid following every new business fashion which you read about in management magazines. If you follow fads, your message will be continually changing. If one week you are telling everyone that TQM is the future of the business, and next week it's re-engineering, no-one is going to take you or your initiatives seriously.

Be honest and realistic

People aren't stupid. If business is bad, the people who work for you will probably know before you do. There is little use in trying to put a brave face on things and give them good news rather than the bad news they can see all round them. They want the truth so they know where they stand. If you are blindly optimistic you will inevitably have created expectations. When your optimism is proved to be completely groundless you have a lot of explaining to do and a great deal of trust to earn. Good news is the preserve of politicians; reality is the only currency of business.

It is especially important to keep customers fully informed. If you are going to deliver something late you have to prepare them for the bad news. You could invent an excuse, but it is preferable to keep them informed throughout so that they know early on that you are going to be late and so they understand the reasons behind your lateness.

Be well prepared

Some people can get on their feet and make inspiring speeches filled with wit, information and inspiration. But for every brilliant speaker there are thousands of tongue-tied mortals. It is no use pretending that you have the oratorical gifts of Winston Churchill if you can barely string a coherent sentence together. Be realistic; instead of casually assuming you can bluff your way through, do your homework. Plan what you are going to say and pay attention to detail. Don't try to be clever.

Remember charisma isn't always what people want to see and poetry is not what they necessarily want to hear. One chief executive gave a speech to a group of employees which was full of information, but was essentially dull. One of the employees was asked what he thought about the chief executive: 'Terrible at speeches and presentations, but he seems careful and well-organised – I would rather he was running the company than someone who made great speeches.'

Be brief

People tend to have a love affair with their own voice. Communication, however, must be a two-way process. People should be encouraged to ask questions – rather than the obligatory 'any questions?' invitation at the very end. Listening is critical to communicating effectively. Let people have their say – but make sure you have yours.

Use face-to-face communication

Even in the technical age, face-to-face communication remains a key business skill. People may be able to communicate through modems and the like, but the impact of a personal meeting can never be underestimated.

Tailor the message

Different people need to receive the same message in different ways. You must be able to change your presentational style to fit the audience's needs and to use the medium which suits them and your message best. Think what can help you get your message across. Do you really need 165 slides with complex diagrams or could you sum it up in a single diagram?

● Selling

Having the great idea is one thing, selling and marketing it successfully is quite another. This can be extremely daunting. Few people actually enjoy cold-calling. As the failed telephone calls mount, remember that everyone sells something no matter who they are or what they do – a greengrocer sells fruit and vegetables, a consultant sells expertise in a particular area, a doctor sells medical knowledge, a footballer sells the ability to kick a ball and a salesman sells the ability to sell things.

Selling the idea to the bank

The first port of call is often your bank. If you require financial support – an overdraft facility or a loan – the bank will want to know more about your business. The normal way of providing this is through a business plan. This is an important document – and one you need to prepare even if you don't require help from the bank. It maps out what your business will do, who its customers will be, your qualifications and experience to make it successful, and your future plans and anticipated financial needs and targets.

Preparing a business plan

A common mistake is to assume that the business plan must be a large document with copious charts and information to impress. In fact, bankers and venture capitalists are unlikely to be impressed by a meandering book-sized plan. They want to see and hear that you have thought about your idea and why you believe the business will be successful. The business plan should, therefore, be less than ten pages – though you should have other documents and information to back it up if necessary.

The business plan should include:

- **The business**: what it will do and the people involved
- **The market**: an overview of the market you wish to compete in
- **Customers**: identification of who the likely customers are and how you will market your product or service to them
- **Competitive advantage**: why your proposition is different and will attract customers
- **Long-term plans**: what are your aims and targets over the first few years (up to five years). This should include detailed projections of profits, market share, sales and investment needs

It is important to take time over your business plan. It must be highly persuasive – it must look good, professional, serious and confident. It must show that you mean business.

Read on

Ron Johnson, *The Perfect Business Plan*, Century Business, London, 1993

Making selling work

What are you selling? It may be a mass-produced part for a machine which appears inconsequential when it is fitted to the multi-million pound machines of your customers. But it is more than that. The minute part you make in batches of 250,000 is crucial to making your customer's machine work. Consultant Ken Langdon explains: 'Customers do not buy a tie because it has bright colours, is made of silk or is washable at 40 degrees. They do so because they imagine how people will think of them when they are wearing it. They do not buy a computer because it has a fast processor, a colour screen or an adjustable keyboard. They buy a computer because it is going to reduce the amount of finished goods stock they are holding and thereby improve their profitability. Neither can it be forgotten that customers have a choice. They can always buy someone else's product.'

Selling revolves around clearly defining the benefits to the customer of buying your particular product or service. You are not selling a small inconsequential part, but something which is essential for the smooth running of your customer's business. Selling must be based round the needs and aspirations of customers. If you forget the customer, you can forget the sale. You can sell customers things they don't really want or need, but you can do so only for a very short time. If you continue, you will soon run out of customers. If the customer doesn't trust you, he or she will simply not buy. If you have tried to sell them something which they don't need or which doesn't work, their trust is liable to be extremely limited. Sales people aren't – or shouldn't be – irritants or bullies. In fact, research shows that in 83 per cent of cases, customers actually *like* the sales person.

Talk to the right person

Making contact with the right person is essential. It may be that your existing contacts allow you direct access to the person or people who will be buying your product. But for many people, finding the right person with the buying power is hard work and involves persistence as you negotiate the maze of a large organisation's hierarchy and telephone system. In the desperate search for positive responses, it is tempting to talk to someone whose views don't really matter, but who is interested and positive. This wastes time and money. You have to find the right person – the one who commands the purse strings.

In achieving the right level of contact, you need a deep knowledge of the marketplace and of customers, and have to be able to talk at the right level – whether it is easy or not. At different levels, places and companies you will need to adopt different approaches. The chairman of a large company requires a different approach from a stationery buyer because they will be looking for different things from you, your business and the product or service.

Know the product

Selling revolves around simplicity. What you are selling has to appear blissfully simple, the solution to the customer's worries and problems. For the small business man or woman this is often easier said than done. If you actually invented the product it is easy to become carried away, to wax lyrical on its many complex merits.

'In theory it is impossible to know too much about the product you are selling. But you have to emphasise the *application* of the product rather than its manufacture,' says Ken Langdon.

Customers are unlikely to be interested in the remarkable technical innovations which have made the product possible. But if you have just introduced a lifetime guarantee, this is likely to be significant to them.

Striking a balance is not easy. In preparation you need to run through as many possible scenarios as you can imagine.

Think of the likely questions a customer will have about your product or service and think about your responses. The guide to all of this must be to match the needs and aspirations of the customer with what the product or service can provide.

Be persistent

'You have to keep plugging away. No matter who you are you have to be continually attracting new customers,' says consultant Tim Foster. 'You are often dealing with customers and clients who work for large organisations. You have to be aware of their agenda. While the self-employed are accustomed to taking risks, people in organisations are often risk-averse. They are fearful of being fired or made redundant. How the hell do you get work from people who aren't willing to take a risk?'

Selling checklist [1]

The customer

- Would the customer really benefit from your product or service?
- In what way would they benefit? In the short term? In the long term?
- Are you able to identify all the key people in the company?
- Are they the decision-makers?
- How much sales effort does the customer demand?

Finance

- Does the customer have the money available in a budget?
- Does the customer have a rough expectation of cost?

---

[1] Many ideas in this checklist are adapted from Ken Langdon's innovative work on selling and managing a salesforce which are distilled in *Key Accounts Are Different*, Pitman Publishing, London, 1985

Timescale

- Have the key people agreed on a decision date?
- Is there an agreed implementation timescale?

Solution

- Is your solution valid?
- Can you deliver it when the customer wants in the numbers required?
- Can you support your solution?

Competition

- Do you have an advantage?
- Do you fully understand what they are offering and at what price?

Clarity

Have you made it clear;

- what the customer will receive;
- when they will receive it?

Have you clarified who is the main point of contact:

- in your business, and;
- in the customer's?

> **Four routes to increased sales**
>
> The American management thinker, Igor Ansoff, has identified four basic ways in which sales can be increased:
>
> 1 Selling more existing products in existing markets. This is the low risk strategy, probably revolving around a marketing campaign or other promotion.
>
> 2 Selling new or modified products to existing customers.
>
> 3 Selling existing products in new markets or to new customers.
>
> 4 Selling new products to new markets. This is the area of highest risk.

Building sales

Having achieved a sale in a particular organisation you then have to develop the business. This can be done in a number of ways.

Developing contacts

Do you have regular business meetings at all levels with:

- Senior management?
- High level within the product users?
- High and wide at technical level?
- Where necessary in Central Purchasing?

Measuring customer satisfaction

- Do you have an agreed measure of customer satisfaction with the customer?
- Do you deliver what you promised on time and within budget?

- Does the product give the expected up-time?
- Where problems occur are they fixed quickly?
- Are you supporting the customer properly where appropriate?

Strategic fit

- Are you thoroughly aware of your company's product strategy and can you articulate it to your customer?
- Does your plan fit in with your company's strategy?
- Is there a connection between your plan and your customer's overall strategy?
- Can you see the connection between your plan and some customer critical success factor(s)?
- Can you see the connection between your plan and a change in a crucial customer performance indicator(s)?

Keeping up to date with the competition

- Are you aware of the strengths and weaknesses of the main competitors you are facing?

Purchasing's Four Os

Objects	What are customers going to do with the product or service after they buy it?
Objectives	Why will the customers buy the product or service; how is it going to help them meet their business objectives?
Organisation	Who in the customer company will actually buy the product?
Operations	What are the systems and procedures the customer follows in buying anything?

- Are you aware of your company's strengths and weaknesses in relation to the main competitors?
- How vulnerable is your installed base to competitive attack?
- Are you seen as price competitive and value for money?

● Marketing

'Small business marketing is the vehicle of entrepreneurial success where operations put the customer first. Small business management needs to establish the customer profile in the target market, analyse the competition and regularly evaluate capacity to guarantee the consistent delivery of quality products/services more effectively – and then efficiently – than the competition,' says Manchester Business School's small business expert, Panikkos Poutziouris.

Purchasing has four Os, marketing is blessed with four **P**s – **P**roduct, **P**rice, **P**romotion and **P**lace. To these can be added two other **P**s – **P**eople and **P**rocesses. The most difficult and contentious is price. For the small business man or woman finding the right price is notoriously taxing. If you are making a physical product it is comparatively straightforward – you can work out costs and production times so you have an accurate idea of your profit margins. For service businesses it is a little more difficult. You are selling your expertise, experience and time. In such cases there are a number of helpful rules of thumb.

- Learn from others: you may be able to find out how much competitors charge. This should help you gauge how much you can afford to charge.
- There may be accepted or set pricing structures: for example, there may be a union rate which can be taken as a minimum.
- Do not undercharge in the expectation of future work. If you set a price which is relatively low for your first piece of work,

the customer's expectations will be set. If you double the price for the next job, they are unlikely to be pleased. It is better to set a realistic and fair figure and attempt to stick to it. Undercharging can also send the wrong messages – if everyone else is charging £500 a day and you quote a figure of £100 a day, you are running the risk of looking amateurish. However, this does not mean that you should quote astronomical figures in order to give the impression of professionalism.

- The most important thing is to have thought carefully about how much you want to charge and what your lowest possible figure for the work could be. Do not go below this figure.

But you still have to be flexible. Every job is unique. The circumstances will differ slightly. The customer is different and has different expectations. Their timescales will also vary – you may be able to charge a premium for quick delivery.

In other aspects of marketing, small businesses are confronted with their limitations – and their potential. First the limitations. Small businesses can rarely find the money necessary to indulge in expensive marketing campaigns. Nor can they change direction as quickly as large companies. They are less likely to have the necessary in-house knowledge and expertise. If the market fundamentally shifts, smaller companies can be left high and dry. Alternatively, smaller companies are often competing with firms of a similar size. Their competitiveness is built around sound long-term relationships with customers. If new competitors appear they can more easily innovate or target small parts of a particular market, niches.

Niche strategies target, or create, gaps in the market which larger firms find unsuitable or simply too small to bother with. If a small business is concentrating on a niche market its marketing strategy may emphasise quality and meeting the specialised needs of customers rather than price.

Despite the competitive advantage of their marketing operations in terms of flexibility, innovation and personalised service, small businesses have to be on their guard. They have to develop sales continually, know the market and be proactive.

Develop sales continually

If a small business discovers a lucrative niche in a market it will enjoy initial success. The trouble is that niche markets can be too localised or specialised – to expand elsewhere becomes a huge and expensive risk. For small companies developing new markets is costly and risky. The only way forward is to return to the basics and carefully consider another market which fits the business's skills and experience.

Know the market

You may not have the time, skills or the energy to monitor and utilise market information. Market research to establish the customer profile, source and form of competition and identify market trends is often beyond the financial and administrative base of small firms. Even so, it is still essential. There are an array of publicly available sources of information – libraries are a rich source of information and data. You may also find useful information and assistance from trade associations, unions, the Chamber of Commerce, professional bodies, small business campaigning groups and national organisations.

Be proactive

Small firms often lack the qualified technical specialists and financial resources to support a formal research and development programme to produce innovative products. In response to competitive pressure from mainly larger counterparts, often backed by costly advertising campaigns, small firms target localised and specialised markets with high quality, customised products/services.

The niche trap

If you corner a small but lucrative market, what's next?

Forget expansion, stick to the successful niche might be one line of advice. This runs the risk of stagnation. There is usually a time limit to how long you can mine the rewards of a niche market. Competitors may suddenly emerge, leaving you with no choice but to look or move elsewhere. Sticking with what you've got can be a dangerous option.

We've mastered the niche, let's tackle the rest of the market is the next argument. This, unfortunately, does not necessarily follow. You may be the UK leader in supplying the Brazilian coffee industry with an important device. This does not mean that the same device is essential in Kenya or another coffee-producing country – they might not need it or might have a perfectly effective local alternative.

There must be similar markets elsewhere, let's find them runs a third argument. You might spend a long time looking – by then the company could be struggling.

Which other markets are our competitors in? Let's follow them. This sounds persuasive. What's good enough for them might well be good enough for you. But being a follower rather than a leader is a perilous course.

Understanding your market

Customers

- *location* street, village, town, postcode, area, country, region, UK/international
- *people* social information about relative spending power and spending habits of different groups of society
- *businesses* size, turnover, type.

What are the needs and priorities of customers, eg reliability, price, quality?

1

2

3

4

Target markets

Describe different groups of customers – these can be divided by the product required, location, industry, etc.

1

2

3

4

5

6

Target markets

Describe different groups of customers – these can be divided by the product required, location, industry, etc.

1

2

3

4

5

6

Now, how large a part of the business would you like each to be?

1

> 2
>
> 3
>
> 4
>
> **Promotion**
>
> Which promotional methods are suitable for each group of customers?
>
> ☐ advertising (newspaper, trade journals, TV, radio)
> ☐ leaflets
> ☐ brochures
> ☐ direct mail
> ☐ others

Further Information

Institute of Practitioners in Advertising
44 Belgrave Square, London SW1X 8QS
Telephone: 0171-235 7020

● Negotiating

Negotiating is a vital, often unacknowledged, part of business. In one form or another negotiating accounts for large amounts of our time. As a skill which can be enhanced and developed, negotiating is all but ignored. Yet, by developing skills which allow for full and complete negotiations – rather than overly quick or confrontational ones – managers can achieve results which are mutually beneficial.

'Many people become worried about the prospect of having to conduct a negotiation. It seems from the outside to be a process shrouded in mystery, performed by the expert. In fact, it is no such thing, as most people are involved in negotiating on a daily basis, and have been ever since they swapped conkers or lollipops,' says Jane Hodgson, author of *Thinking on Your Feet in Negotiations*. 'Looking at it as a problem solving rather than point winning exercise, preparing thoroughly and imaginatively, and using some simple skills and strategies can help to ensure that agreements are made which are not only satisfactory to both parties immediately, but stand the test of time. Settlements which are reached quickly, with a superficial compromise agreed, have a huge potential for breaking down because of misunderstandings, cosmetic consensus, or a failure to explore the issues thoroughly enough.'

Starting a business, you may well find yourself negotiating with the bank manager, suppliers, customers, employees and even your family. Skilled negotiators have a number of characteristics:

- **Seeking information** Skilled negotiators ask for more than twice as much information as average negotiators, asking questions to obtain essential information with which to bargain, and as a way of controlling the discussion, avoiding disagreements or reducing the other party's thinking time.

- **Testing, understanding and summarising** They check a statement or proposal is understood, and then summarise it. This clarifies things and reduces the potential for misunderstandings. In contrast, less effective negotiators are keen to reach agreement and tend to leave ambiguous points to be cleared up later. Unfortunately, this often means that they are never cleared up at all and, when it comes to implementation, more negotiation is required.

- **Using language** Skilled negotiators are adept at giving advance warning about what's coming next. They make suggestions rather than direct, confrontational, questions.

Rather than asking: 'What is the deadline for this?', they would say: 'Can I ask you a question? What is the deadline for this?' They also use phrases such as 'I'd like to make a suggestion' rather than simply telling the other side what their solution is. These may seem like semantic, time-wasting techniques, but they slow the pace of the negotiation down so that issues are thought about and, eventually, resolved. Similarly, skilled negotiators don't rush in and say 'I disagree'. Instead, they rationally and logically go through their case, before concluding that the force of the argument as it stands forces them to disagree.

- ***Allowing feelings to show*** Skilled negotiators allow their feelings to show. This appears remarkably candid, but they are less likely to divulge cut and dried figures. They are human, but careful with it.

Negotiating is a fine art. There are a number of common mistakes:

- ***Blowing your own trumpet*** Phrases such as 'reasonable offer', 'generous terms', 'fair', 'honest', 'impartial', etc. can cause trouble. If you describe your offer as 'reasonable' you are suggesting that any rational individual would recognise it as such. Praising your own behaviour (and insinuating the other side is ignorant or less reasonable) is unlikely to be productive. Any industrial dispute featured on the TV news usually includes such self-congratulation.

- ***Being overly aggressive*** Negotiations are often approached as wars, but being overly aggressive and continually being on the offensive is self-defeating. Poor negotiators are continually attacking. Each new proposal is greeted with a counter-proposal. This simply puts the other side on the defensive, then they too are likely to attack back. The result is a pointless escalation. In contrast, effective negotiators are adept at attacking at the right time and of defusing situations when they appear ready to escalate.

- **Too many arguments**   A simple message backed with a small number of logical supporting points is more persuasive than a large number of arguments. If you are negotiating keep to the three or four core points. If you bring in peripheral arguments you may well find they are your weakest and can be exploited.

- **Look to the future**   Negotiators need to look to the future. It is little use stitching together a desperate eleventh hour compromise if, two weeks later, you have to start again. Agreements need to focus on long-term relationships and implementation.

Read on

Jane Hodgson, *Thinking on Your Feet in Negotiations*, FT/Pitman, London, 1994

Donald Hendon and Rebecca Hendon, *How to Negotiate Worldwide*, Gower, Aldershot, 1989

● Sweat and obsession

> **"Obsession does not guarantee success. On the other hand a lack of obsession does guarantee failure."**
>
> Tom Peters

'Obsession does not guarantee success. On the other hand a lack of obsession does guarantee failure,' says management guru Tom Peters in his blockbuster *Liberation Management*. Like it or not, obsession has become an integral part of running a business. Indeed, obsessives are all around us; Eurobond dealers who work 12 hours a day fuelled by a concoction of adrenaline, caffeine and pure fear; factory managers who stay long after everyone else has left, to pore over the day's production figures; sales managers who spend hours in their cars listening to tapes on how to be more successful. For them business has become much more than work, fun or financial gain – but an end in itself.

Obsessives expect others to follow suit. They regard their obsessiveness as a source of inspiration. 'I believe if someone comes to work for me I pay them well and expect them to give me their absolute,' says one senior manager, 'I don't believe you should tell people to do things. You should ask them and they should expect to come in early every morning and go home late at night and just work and work because they enjoy doing it.'

If obsessive managers could take a step back it would be easy for them to recognise the unhealthy side of their obsession. It dominates their life to the detriment of family, friends and fun. At work it may well cloud their judgement – often they are so obsessed they are incapable of being objective.

Working for an obsessive boss poses unique problems and is rarely compatible with job security. 'Obsession is where commonsense bites the corporate dust,' says a manager who has worked for two bosses he identifies as obsessive. 'I did not go along with the obsession so I was quickly shown the door.'

'But the people I worked with carried on working an obsessive number of hours and did not question the boss's demanding habits. To the obsessive boss no-one else's world matters. If you point out, as I did, that their decisions are not rational but based on obsessive prejudice, you can guarantee fireworks.'

The dividing line between commitment (healthy and outward-looking) and obsession (unhealthy and inward-looking) is a thin one. It is a precarious balancing act. Running your own business you need to be extraordinarily focused and thorough in what you do. But paradoxically, you cannot afford to be narrow in your outlook. Companies need a combination of extremely focused managers and ones with more of an entrepreneurial outlook taking in the broader picture.

Having sailed across the Atlantic, Jonathan Jeffes knows a thing or two about obsession. Now managing director of Westward Training and Development, he believes that companies are becoming better at identifying obsessives, whether they are empire-builders or obsessively competitive and redirecting their energies. 'People are often obsessed with the wrong thing – how many hours they work on a particular task,' he says.

'Obsession', like anything else, needs to be channelled in the right direction. If it isn't you end up with people doing their own thing for their own ends rather than working as a team.'

Bob Kaplan of the US Center for Creative Leadership, prefers not to use the word obsessive with its negative connotations. In his book, *Beyond Ambition*, Kaplan came up with the word 'expansive' to sum up the obsessive striving of many managers. 'Executives desire a sense not merely of adequacy but of high personal worth, and they seek it not by doing an acceptable job, but by doing an exceptional job,' he says. 'Expansive executives see themselves, perhaps unconsciously, as heroes. Like heroes, they want to execute some masterstroke, or accomplish prodigious amounts of work or adhere to the highest standards.'

Obsession is a recurring theme in the way heroes and antiheroes are portrayed in all walks of life. The actor Alan Bates has said: 'Everyone who is any good is obsessive.' Films are full of obsessives who should really be in therapeutic clinics – from Indiana Jones to Gordon Gekko in *Wall Street*. Perhaps the most obsessive individuals are those with their own companies. For them there is no escape. 'If you are not obsessed with your idea, there is no point in starting a business,' says Tim Scott of the Business Founder's Bureau. 'But if you are to overcome the myriad of obstacles ahead, establish credibility and succeed, you have to temper your obsession with reality. Obsessives need a touchstone – often their partner – to bring them back to earth. Otherwise, they end up being blind to any of the pitfalls.'

For the self-employed, obsession is paradoxically, often essential. Again the balance is delicate. Bank managers are likely to be more reticent about lending money to an obsessed zealot with a distant gleam in his eye than to someone obsessed with achieving quality products at competitive prices.

If obsession is to work for you, it has to be harnessed to business objectives. It can be a great driving force, enabling everyday crises to be swept aside. But if it is allowed to develop unchecked, obsession can be disastrous, no matter what the business.

> **The problem is a simple one – cash does not flow. Instead a trickle of money is received while a deluge is spent.**

4

Managing the money

● The financial obstacle course

Business boils down to money. People starting their own business may do so with idealistic notions of revolutionising their lifestyle or doing something they enjoy, but these objectives require that the idea and the business actually make a profit. Managing your money is one of the cornerstones of business success. When you start out, finance can seem straightforward but the bigger you become, the more complex the financial demands.

Some manage to keep it simple. Denise O'Donoghue, managing director of TV production company Hat Trick Productions which makes 'Whose Line Is It Anyway?' and 'Drop The Dead Donkey', says the company has never borrowed money. 'I have a very domestic attitude to running a company. Keep overheads low and don't compromise on product.' This is a useful philosophy to have (Margaret Thatcher went one stage further and applied domestic prudence to the economy of a country) but rather difficult to implement when you are juggling money in the early stages of your business development. It is very easy to start off with noble intentions, only to quickly find that they are not the best way to make a success of the business.

Hard and fast rules – such as refusing to contemplate borrowing – are all well and good, but can be difficult to adhere to. If you rule out borrowing, how can you fund the expensive machines which you must have to stay in business? The onus must be on flexibility laced with caution, professional advice and commonsense.

The financial obstacles facing small businesses are many and varied. None can be ignored – overlooking them can have serious repercussions.

The personal and family cost

A survey of 700 small firms carried out by the National Federation of Enterprise Agencies and *The Observer* newspaper found that 58 per cent of businesses said that the single largest source of funding when starting up their business was their own money and savings. A further 13 per cent cited family and friends as the largest source of support. Bank loans were used by 12 per cent.

There are heavy personal and social costs in the start-up, survival and growth stages of a family business for entrepreneurs, their families, relatives and friends. In the first instance, companies often rely on money from the owner, his or her family and sometimes helpful friends. This can be an onerous burden. It is one thing explaining to the bank manager that business is not as good as anticipated and you require a bigger overdraft, quite another to ask a friend or family backer for another injection of cash.

While it may be extremely useful to receive financial support from family and friends, both sides need to treat it as a business arrangement. If the terms aren't clear to either side, there is a strong chance of confusion or arguments. It may be worthwhile, therefore, to draw up some sort of legal agreement or at least put the expectations of both sides down in writing. This can save on wrangles later on.

Matching financial arrangements to changing conditions

Nothing stays the same. Though you may start the business on a shoestring, at any time you may need to borrow money or change the way the business is financed. Very often this is a crucial stumbling block to a business developing successfully.

The small business can't win. In order to grow it might be vital that you buy a new machine, another computer or another premises. This may require more money than you have at your disposal. As a small business, the proportionate increase is likely to be large and your ability to receive financial support is limited. The catch-22 is often that to develop you need capital investment; but your very smallness is off-putting to potential backers.

Another common obstacle – part of the same catch-22 – is that you don't have enough assets to secure loan finance. Again, your very smallness is a handicap. Small businesses are often undercapitalised. To back their loans, financial institutions will insist on some form of collateral. To secure loan finance the small firm owner provides personal collateral. This may be in the form of a guarantee or property deed. While this may secure extra finance, it also may erode limited liability and greatly adds to your personal financial risk.

The conservative nature of banks

Banks are hardly renowned for their propensity to hand out money to any bright young entrepreneur who happens to come along. Indeed, they are regularly criticised for their lack of support for people with great ideas who need financial backing. Undoubtedly, they are cagey and suspicious, conservative to a fault, interested in backing guaranteed winners rather than rank outsiders. As a result, to receive financial support from banks, you must put across a highly persuasive case. Their refusal to provide essential finance can sound the death-knell for the business – no matter how good the idea.

The culture of your business

As if these problems weren't enough, they are often worsened by the attitudes and company culture created by the business owner. If you start a business with nothing and build it up, it can seem like a loss of face to go to a bank to ask for a loan. Often this justifiable pride prevents opportunities for future growth being taken. But all you have to lose is your pride – and you may gain a larger and more profitable business.

Similarly, small businesses can be suspicious of bringing in specialists to help them with their finances. Initially, it may be comparatively straightforward to do your accounts and finances. You may feel quite confident of being able to handle it. As the business grows, however, so does the financial complexity. At this stage it is worth having an accountant.

It is important to have an accountant. An accountant can make your life a lot easier though it may be an extra expense you believe you can do without. They can cut through apparently intractable problems, simply through their experience in knowing who to contact and what to do. Using an accountant shifts the burden of dealing with the Inland Revenue to someone who knows the ins and outs of their complicated procedures.

It is worth shopping around, asking other people which accountants they use, so that you find someone you feel comfortable with and who is happy to deal with your business. Accountants can be relatively inexpensive – the expense depends on how complex your business is and, therefore, how much time they need to spend on your accounts.

● Money for starters

The National Federation of Enterprise Agencies and *The Observer* survey identified funding as the single largest constraint in setting up a business named by 52 per cent of the businesses. The second ranking constraint, with a mere 14 per cent, was marketing.

How much money you will need to start your business depends on the nature of the business. Some businesses demand very little in the way of equipment. A journalist who becomes self-employed, for example, will probably need a telephone, fax machine, a computer and little else. Consultants are also able to set up their businesses with little or no need for costly investments in technological equipment.

Some of the world's biggest and most successful companies started with virtually no finance – Apple Computers began in a garage with $1,300. Other businesses require investment and financial support long before they can actually begin to sell their product or service. Technical or innovative products may require *seed capital* – finance for the early stages of research and development. Pilot and naval engineer Clive Linnell is developing a new form of helicopter, the Heli D Wing. Simply getting his innovative idea to 'a proof of concept' prototype requires £800,000.

Planning and monitoring your start-up expenses is complicated. Be careful. As you set up the business it can be quite difficult to keep track of where all the money is going. You may think that your high expenses are caused by the new furniture you are buying, but it may be that your actual running costs are too high. Also beware of hidden costs. These can come in many different guises – connection costs, added extras you don't really need, delivery charges, charges for speedy delivery. It is very easy to underestimate start-up costs when you are naturally enthusiastic and optimistic, but:

- ***Shop around for suppliers*** There are a myriad of special deals available, many of them targeted at small businesses. It is worth reminding suppliers that if your business takes off they may be able to expect larger orders in the future.

- ***Control costs*** Be clear what you do and do not need. Always bear in mind the customer. 'I have retained a strong mental image of who my customers will be,' says Pentacle founder, Eddie Obeng. 'Buying the furniture and computer equipment, I have actually thought of a particular person who I have in my mind as a likely customer. I ask what he would think of a particular purchase?

   'I started out mapping the start-up costs, but found that there were too many variations and additions to do it accurately. Indeed, I have consciously not skimped on things like furniture – I want them to last and to impress my clients.'

- **Get details in writing** It is important that you know exactly what you are buying, how much it will cost and when it will be delivered. If you have details in writing you are in a stronger position when your desk or computer fails to arrive.

- **talk to others** to discover what hidden costs they encountered. Other people in similar – or even completely different – businesses will be able to tell you the problems they encountered and how they solved them.

As a *contingency plan* it is advisable to add as much as a third to your estimates. This should cover the additional costs which invariably surface and mean that your finances may be more realistic.

Capital costs

What equipment do you need now?

Item   Approximate cost   Business benefits

What equipment will you need next year?

Item   Approximate cost   Business benefits

What equipment will you need within five years?

Item   Approximate cost   Business benefits

● Sources of support

There are a surprisingly large number of possible sources of financial advice and support. Family and friends and your bank may be the first ports of call, but they need not be the last. It is worth looking into some of the other possibilities as they may offer financing options which are more appropriate to your business.

Government support

There are a great many government-sponsored support schemes, many of which offer financial assistance in the early stages of a business's life. These include the following.

SMART An annual competition open to individuals or firms with less than 50 employees. It aims to stimulate highly innovative but also highly marketable technology. Entrants with the best commercially viable ideas are awarded up to £45,000 towards the first year's development costs. The most promising winners may be awarded up to £60,000 to take their ideas closer to the marketplace. SMART has been running since 1986 and is administered on a regional basis by the DTI.

SPUR is a scheme to help firms or groups with up to 500 employees in total, to develop new products and processes which involve a significant technological advance for the industry concerned. SPUR offers flat rate grants of 30 per cent towards the eligible costs, up to a maximum of £150,000.

Regional Innovation Grants are available to firms of less than 25 employees in specified development areas. These offer 50 per cent of the agreed cost of an innovation up to a maximum of £25,000.

The Loan Guarantee Scheme (from the DTI) is designed to assist viable small firms who are unable to raise conventional finance due to lack of security or track record. By providing a government guarantee, the scheme encourages banks and other financial institutions to lend where they would normally be unwilling to do so. The Scheme guarantees 70 per cent of loans between £5,000 and £100,000. The guarantee is 85 per cent of up to £250,000 for small firms which have been in business for two years or more. Applications for the Scheme are made through the 20 lenders taking part; these include High Street banks and a number of other organisations.

Further information on the Loan Guarantee Scheme can be obtained from the Small Firms Branch of the DTI in Sheffield, Telephone: 01742 597308.

European funding There are now also a large number of European initiatives aiming to encourage small businesses. As these are ever changing and often depend on the location of your business, you need to find out more. The European Commission in London has an Information Centre which should be able to provide details of the the latest programmes. Telephone: 0171-973 1992.

Outside investors

The United Kingdom has the largest venture capital industry outside the United States. Venture capitalists back their hunches with investments in new businesses. Their investments are usually substantial – corner shops need not apply (unless they wish to become Sainsbury's). Competition is also intense. Venture capital companies receive some 50,000 proposals each year of which a mere 600 progress to a conclusion. An estimated 50,000 other business proposals go no further than a refusal from the bank.

Generally, venture capitalists are looking for businesses with high growth potential. They are not looking for short-term returns, but prefer to work with the entrepreneur to secure substantial long-term returns on their investment.

Outside investment can bridge an important gap in your initial finances. For example, when Anita Roddick was putting together money to start her first shop in Brighton she sold a share in the company to a local garage owner for £4,000 – the share is now worth £95 million. The garage owner is one of many people with sometimes possess substantial amounts of money which they would like to invest in new businesses. Research by the ESRC, DTI and NatWest suggests that there are 200,000 to 400,000 informal investors (labelled 'business angels') who would like to invest between £200,000 and £500,000 in unquoted companies.

Outside investors fall into a number of categories.

- **Virgins**   Those with no experience. It may seem a good idea to receive backing from an elderly spinster in Eastbourne who is prepared to lend you her life savings. But it is unlikely that such an investor will be able to offer constructive support or have a full understanding of what they are letting themselves in for. They may begin to fret early on and put pressure on for a return on their investment. Managing them can become as large a headache as managing the business.

- **Wealth-maximisers**   These investors want to make the most of their wealth. Ideally the source of their wealth is a business related in some way to your own.

- **Income-seekers**   Rather than putting their money in building societies these investors seek a steady source of income through investing in a small business. They may become disenchanted when the returns fail to match the consistency or security of those from savings accounts.

- **Corporate venturers**   'Corporate venturing' involves large companies investing in private businesses. While popular in the United States, it is largely untested in the United Kingdom. Engineering company JCB recently invited designers, inventors and companies with under-funded engineering projects to cotact JCB with ideas which required backing. JCB has suggested that up to £1 million could be available. Despite such offers, corporate venturing has a poor track record of converting offers into cash for small businesses.

● ***Entrepreneurs*** These investors make their living from using their instincts to spot business opportunities. Success can depend on establishing a close and mutually beneficial relationship with them. It tends to be highly personal.

Further information

British Venture Capital Association
Telephone: 0171-233 5212

UK Venture Capital Journal, Venture Economic
Telephone: 0171-434 0411

Local Investment Networking Co.
Telephone: 0171-236 3000

Capital Exchange
Telephone: 01432 342484

TecInvest
Telephone: 01606 734288

Venture Capital Report
Telephone: 01491 579999

A booklet, *Finance Without Debt*, is available from the Department of Employment's Small Firms Division
Telephone: 01742 597315

There is also a *Directory of Sources of Venture Capital* which lists 200 organisations offering amounts of venture capital less than £250,000. This is an HMSO publication.

● Dealing with the tax man

Anyone whose job entails taking money from you is automatically associated with a faceless uncaring bureaucracy. This is understandable. Tax offices are generally huge buildings filled with bulging and ragged files. Somewhere, one has your name on. This is not a comforting thought but, unless we believe certain politicians, taxation is unlikely to be abolished.

There is no avoiding dealing with the tax man or woman. Death and taxes are still certainties. In fact, as soon as you begin your business you have to inform your local tax office as well as the local Social Security Office. As a self-employed person you are responsible for your own tax and National Insurance. For those used to working for a company where tax and National Insurance are handled by another department this can be a daunting prospect.

From Day One you have to keep 'full and accurate records and proper accounts'. If your turnover is less than £15,000 you don't have to submit detailed accounts – a summary is acceptable – but you still need to be able to back this up with records of all your business transactions if necessary. The summary should show your turnover, purchases and expenses, and your net profits. It is worth examining the money you spent before actually starting the business. You might be able to claim some tax relief on this if it would have been an allowable expense once your business had started. (This does not, however, apply to capital expenditure.)

Not preparing your accounts means that the Inland Revenue will estimate your income and charge you tax on this amount. This could be way in excess of the amount you actually earned, so it is worthwhile avoiding. Similarly, if you fail to pay your tax on time you begin to pay interest.

If you employ people you may also have to deduct tax and National Insurance under the Pay As You Earn system if the person earns over a certain amount.

The complexity of your accounts depends largely on the complexity of the business. The basic information you need to include is:

- takings
- expenses – all your business expenses including rent, rates, lighting, heating, insurance, repairs to premises, fixtures and fittings, car running costs, gross wages and salaries, stationery, postage, telephone and many more. In

some instances, such as using your car or telephone, there will be a split between personal and business use. You need to keep records so the split between the two can be accurately calculated. If you determine that 60 per cent of your phone calls are for business, then this amount of your bill and rental is a legitimate business expense.

- any private money introduced into the business
- cash taken from the business – the money you have extracted to pay yourself
- details of cheques drawn from your business account and what they were for
- market value of any goods taken from the business if they weren't paid for at the correct retail price
- money owed to you by customers at the end of the accounting period
- amounts owed by you to suppliers.

When the accounting period comes to an end you may well have stocks, raw materials or partly completed work. This needs to be accounted for.

The tax situation changes almost constantly. The basic principles are: be honest, be able to back up figures with receipts and, if you are unsure about something, contact your local Tax Office or your accountant.

Capital allowances

The cost of business machinery or vehicles cannot be treated as a business expense. But you can claim **capital allowances** on such purchases. Claiming capital allowances is a good argument in itself for employing an accountant. Basically you can claim allowances on plant or machinery, such as:

- vans and cars
- computers
- furniture
- ladders
- cement mixers, etc.

You cannot claim for things that you don't use in your business or the cost of buying or improving a building.

Capital allowances allow you to claim for 25 per cent of the value of your expenditure as a business expense. The amount – less the 25 per cent – is then carried forward to the next year. Further information on the full details of capital allowances should be requested from the Inland Revenue.

National Insurance

The self-employed may have to pay two forms of National Insurance: Class 2 (a flat rate) and Class 4 (calculated according to your profits). Class 2 contributions are collected by the Department for Social Security. Class 4 contributions are calculated and assessed by the Inland Revenue and are detailed on your tax assessment. They are paid when you pay your tax. Rates are based on a percentage of annual profits between a lower limit (£6,340 in 1993–94) and an upper limit (£21,840). These limits are altered at budgets.

Further information

For Class 4 contributions, contact your local Tax Enquiry Centre or Tax Office.

Information on Class 2 contributions or other National Insurance problems and queries can be obtained from your local Social Security Office or from:

Class 2 Group, Contributions Agency, DSS Longbenton, Newcastle-upon-Tyne, NE98 1YZ

There is also a Social Security Advice Line on 0800-393539.

● Do you need to be VAT registered?

Value Added Tax (VAT) is a tax on most business transactions. In 1993–94 it brought £39 billion to government coffers. The standard rate of VAT is 17.5 per cent though this is subject to change (usually upwards). The common complaint about VAT is that it turns the business man or woman into an unofficial tax collector. This is largely true. For small businesses VAT is time-consuming – the cost of actually doing all the administration can be larger than the amount you have to pay.

VAT is complicated by the fact that though there is a standard rate, some things are *zero-rated*. These include:

- most food (the exception is 'catering' which includes food you buy in restaurants and take-aways)
- books and newspapers (a matter of continuing debate and lobbying)
- young children's clothing and footwear (difficult to believe if you have to buy shoes for toddlers)
- exports of goods
- prescriptions and aids for the handicapped
- mobile homes and house boats.

It is tempting, therefore, to open a business located on a barge exporting children's clothes.

Other things are *exempt* from VAT. These include such things as insurance, most (but far from all) sales, leases and lettings of land and buildings; and services of doctors and dentists.

You don't have to register for VAT unless your taxable turnover exceeds a certain amount. This amount has steadily increased from £25,400 in 1990 to £37,600 in 1993 and £45,000 in 1994. As soon as your turnover goes above this figure – or is expected to do so – you have to register for VAT.

If you are registered for VAT you include the tax in your invoices. This is your *output* tax. If your customers are VAT registered the tax you charge them is called their *input* tax. This works for people who supply you with materials for your business – if they are VAT registered, things you buy from them are your inputs.

When you receive your VAT return, you simply subtract your input tax from your output tax. The difference must then be paid to Customs and Excise.

It is important to remember that VAT is concerned with your taxable turnover, not your profits. Also, *when* you register is important. If you delay, you may end up having to account for VAT before that date if your turnover was over the limits.

Once registered you need to keep up-to-date and accurate records. You must record all the supplies you make and receive, and a summary of VAT for each period covered by your returns. VAT returns normally arrive every three months.

Further information

Local VAT offices are listed in the phone book under Customs and Excise. They will be able to provide registration forms and leaflets giving full information.

Focused finance

Managing finances successfully requires focus, consistency and communication.

Concentrate on profitability and profit margins

Overtrading is a common cause of business failure. It is caused by the desire to increase turnover at the expense of proper credit control, resulting in late payments and bad debts. Businesses which fail through overtrading have generally overestimated the importance of turnover. How much you sell is *not* the key indicator of whether your business is

The vicious circle

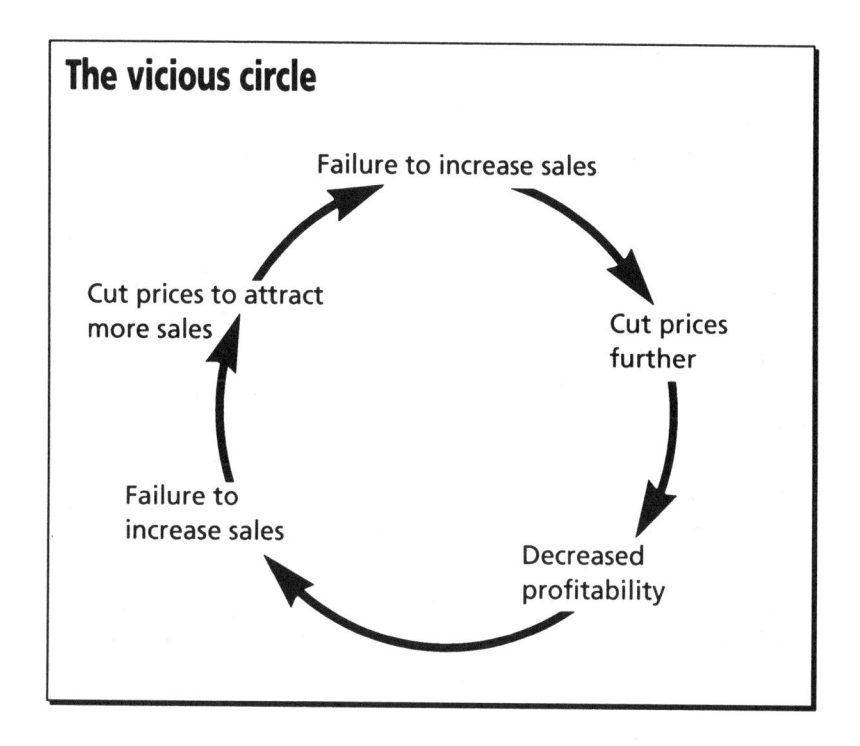

```
        Failure to increase sales
              ↓
Cut prices to attract     Cut prices
more sales                further
      ↑                      ↓
Failure to          Decreased
increase sales      profitability
```

succeeding. It is no use recording steady increases in sales if you are also increasing your overheads so that your profits are low or non-existent. Increased sales often bring with them more substantial costs.

The warning sign is when sales increase and profits remain the same or fall. It is preferable for profits to increase while sales remain level. This suggests that you are controlling costs and generally running your business more efficiently. Of course, ideally both profits and sales increase.

The key, therefore, is to develop your business carefully. Uncontrolled capital expansion is dangerous. Growth is good, but not for its own sake. Any new capital investment must be able to make a financial contribution to the business. Investing in gizmos or technology which don't actually improve your product or service for customers is self-destructive.

Control costs

Cost control is a constant watchword in virtually every organisation. Where it isn't, sooner or later problems can be guaranteed.

Some take it more seriously than others. Major conglomerates, such as Hanson and BTR, have made their reputations and fortunes on their ability to reduce and then control costs in any business they manage. They rarely fail. In your own business there is the added motivation that the money is your own – all you have to do is persuade everyone else in the business to treat your money as if it were their own. This is difficult. You don't want to appear to be a perpetual Scrooge figure, carping over the costs of pencil sharpeners, but you must be constantly aware of where the money is going. This requires tight financial reporting mechanisms. Hanson and BTR are expert at extracting vital information, quickly and efficiently and then, just as important, acting on it. If there are the slightest signs of costs running out of control they act quickly.

Costs are traditionally divided into ones which are *fixed* and those which are *variable*.

Fixed costs are incurred for things that you have to pay for no matter what the parlous state of your finances. They do not go up and down according to the volume you produce. These include:

● insurance

● rent

● rates

● utility bills – lighting, heating, water.

● labour – labour costs once formed the major part of fixed costs, but, with a growing pool of flexible, part-time and temporary workers, they are now likely to be more variable and can be managed according to how busy you are.

Variable costs include buying raw materials, stationery and office supplies. These generally increase as your turnover increases. Controlling them is a crucial factor in increasing your profit margins.

Having examined your cost structure you can break down the total costs of the business into key elements. Once broken down these can be compared with those of competitors, if available, and monitored and measured more easily.

Clearly, it is important that you keep the fixed costs as low as possible and that variable costs are as flexible as possible. This simple intention can be confused by a number of things.

- ***Long-term purchasing contracts*** You need to exercise extreme caution over long-term commitments. In particular, beware of *fixed price contracts*. Long-term fixed price contracts without renegotiation clauses have left many companies facing heavy losses when their own costs mount.

- ***Employing people*** People are expensive assets. The pros and cons of taking on more people needs to be carefully weighed.

- ***Too large premises*** When times are good it is tempting to move to bigger premises. Indeed, you might move into an extremely large building in expectation of your business growing even more. This can prove disastrous.

- ***Too large stocks*** If sales are increasing, it is tempting to produce as many products as you possibly can. You are confident that you will quickly be able to sell your stock. This may happen. But what if business slows down and you are left with a warehouse of products which you simply can't sell? You need to constantly monitor the size and value of your stocks. If you allow them to get out of hand, you may be left with selling them at a loss.

- ***Unrealistic targets*** Many of these problems can be caused by setting targets which are unrealistic. If you are overly optimistic you might produce too many products or move to premises which are larger than your business actually merits. Similarly, overly pessimistic targets can mean that you are simply unable to produce enough to meet orders. It is important to try and be realistic. This is difficult, but can be helped by involving as many people as possible in setting the targets; recruiting a balanced team (a team of hopeless optimists isn't suddenly going to become a group of hard-nosed realists when they look at next year's targets); ensuring that you receive accurate and timely information on all aspects of your business's performance.

Watch the costs, but ...

Inevitably, there is a catch to all this. Minimising costs is important, but can create businesses which are conservative and reactive. They fail to emphasise innovation and react to events rather than taking a lead. Instead of investing in research and development or training and development they concentrate on competing on price alone. This can be short-sighted. Costs must be controlled, but they must also balance the short term and the long term. If you control costs tightly in the short term, you may create a situation in the long term where your products have failed to move on with the changing needs of customers; your people haven't developed appropriate skills; and you are regarded as a business which is more interested in price than producing quality goods or services.

Manage cash flow and control credit

Cash flow is one of the great imponderables of the business world. For the self-employed it is usually nightmarish. The problem is a simple one – cash does not flow. Instead a trickle of money is received while a deluge is spent.

Small businesses are often either poor at credit management – giving people too much credit and collecting debts slowly – or don't manage it at all. The cash flow cycle can frequently lead undercapitalised firms into situations of overtrading, poor liquidity and mismanagement of credit. Poor cash flow often persists even when the business is apparently trading successfully. You can have a book full of orders and a factory running to full capacity and still have insufficient money to pay the wages. This can be caused by misallocating funds. If you don't have a great deal of cash and choose to send all your managers on an expensive training course, or choose that particular time to buy a new machine, you can encounter difficulties. For the small business intent on balancing short-term and long-term needs there may not be a great deal of room for manoeuvre.

The Forum of Private Businesses estimates that United Kingdom businesses are owed £20 billion in overdue debt. There are few signs of any legislation to enforce prompt payment, though the EC is considering introducing a statutory right to interest on unpaid debts.

The nature of the problem varies from business to business. A market garden, for example, does a lot of its business with farmers. Its customers are in the habit of not paying until they return for their next order – this may be in six months or even a year. In the meantime, the market garden has paid for the trees, sold them and still has no money until the customer deigns to make an appearance.

A freelance writer suffers from similar but slightly different problems. Magazines commission articles, a writer delivers and then often has to wait until the article is published before receiving payment. This can mean a wait of many months.

Big businesses are often among the worst payers. Accounts departments are labyrinths around which your humble invoice is endlessly circulated. Straight answers are hard to come by; cheques are invariably waiting to be signed or in the post. The only thing you can do when you are chasing unpaid invoices is make sure you talk to the right person; take their name; pin them down to a time and a date when the cheque will be posted; and then ring again when it fails to arrive.

To some extent the problem is insoluble. If you deal with a large company which is a notoriously slow payer and yet a valuable customer, do you really want to pester your chief contact to push your invoice through? You probably don't; you fear that pestering will create annoyance, and an annoyed customer might overlook you next time. Often small firms offer credit as part of the marketing mix in order to safeguard customer loyalty. On the other hand, you have actually done the work, delivered it on time and are charging a remarkably competitive price.

It is best to make it clear from the start what your payment terms actually are: if you expect payment within 30 days, say so. If it is a large order perhaps suggest that you are paid in instalments.

Be legal

There were a number of well-recorded cases in the 1980s of entrepreneurs whose enthusiasm got the better of them. (This is a polite way of explaining that they broke the law repeatedly and cheated to get ahead.) Such tactics may well work in the short term, but there are a large number of people who are likely to quickly discover any illegal or improper behaviour. It isn't worth it!

Some businesses need to be licensed before they can begin to operate. These include credit companies, anywhere selling alcohol, financial services companies, driving schools and many more.

Use technology

In the area of financial management, technology has undoubtedly made life a great deal easier for small businesses. There are a myriad of accounting packages available. All, inevitably, promise to make your life easier and the monitoring of where the money goes straightforward. The only trouble is their sheer profusion. There are, for example, over 200 accountancy software products currently on the market. For the larger business there are Oracle, SAP, QSP and packages from Dun and Bradstreet. These usually run on mainframe computers so are not suitable for business start-ups. Lower down the scale, for companies with turnovers between £500,000 and £5 million there are products such as Pegasus Senior, Multisoft Prestige and Sage Sovereign.

For the smaller company the choice is even larger. Among the leaders are Sage Sterling, Sage Moneywise and Microsoft Money. The latter is as comprehensive as the small business probably needs in its early days. It enables you to work out VAT, make budgets and track them against optimistic scenarios. There are other accounting systems which are based on Windows – WinAccs, which has been going since 1988, is aimed at small businesses and can be integrated with a Windows-based payroll package, WinPay, and software for job costing.

● The route to financial fiasco

"Financial disasters usually go hand in hand with basic errors of managerial judgement."

Financial disasters usually go hand in hand with basic errors of managerial judgement. Most commonly these include:

● *Inaccurate or untimely information* Poor or non-existent management information is the most common cause of company failure.

● *Failure to respond to a changing environment* The inability to react to changes in the overall economic situation or indeed to changes in the patterns of demand for the company's product has sunk many businesses.

● *Dependence on a handful of key customers or suppliers* Without a reasonable client or supplier base, the loss of a major client or supplier can create serious difficulties.

● *Increased competition* Companies which are unable to

respond to increased competition in terms of product quality and price do not survive.

- **Failure to mature**   The failure to develop a management team which can oversee the business throughout all stages of its development can lead to premature collapse.

- **Extravagant executive lifestyle**   When cost cutting is needed, management costs must take their share of the pain. If the management is dedicated to extravagance they are unlikely to be prepared to make the necessary sacrifices. Common signs of this are: inflated salaries; upgrading company cars; glossy annual reports; move to a new office building more in keeping with the business's stature; perks for managers and their spouses.

"... the old stereotype of an office is fast approaching extinction – except in television comedies ...."

⑤ Where you work

Where you work is a critical factor in how efficiently you work and how customers and others perceive your business. In some businesses location is everything – if you open a shop, for example, the top priority must be to find the right premises. If you are tucked away round a corner passers-by might be in short supply. It is always worth spending a few hours counting the number of people who walk past. Location can, for some, be unimportant. Thanks to technology a freelance trainer or computer programmer can work almost anywhere. For other businesses there is a wide range of choice. Indeed, the choice can be bewildering – do you want somewhere small to reflect your initial projected level of business or do you need somewhere larger for when you meet your planned targets in six months? Do you need a unit or an entire factory? Do you need one office or a suite of offices?

To a large extent it is a lottery. If you are hugely successful you may well find yourself in a building which is too cramped. But you don't want to be desperately seeking orders as your large office or factory is lying empty and idle. Caution is probably the best advice. After all, some of the world's most successful companies started in inauspicious surroundings. A garage in Palo Alto, California, is now registered as Californian historical landmark number 976 'The birthplace of Silicon Valley'. It was here in 1938 that William Hewlett and David Packard began Hewlett-Packard.

Again the two crucial elements must be your customers and finance. When selecting the location and type of premises you must bear in mind:

- **location of customers** If you set up a long way from customers you will incur extra delivery costs and may lose out through being distant from the people who matter.

- **location of suppliers** If you rely on a small number of suppliers who are based in a particular area it is unwise to move to somewhere hundreds of miles away.

- **your current location** Do you need to move and, if so, why?

- **competition** Where are your competitors located and why?

As small businesses tend to rely more on co-operation with other firms and developing subcontracting networks, it is important that the location is right. A number of other elements need to be borne in mind:

- The nature of the business
- Technical matters (such as fitting machinery in)
- Business aspirations – If you know that to make a profit you need to make so many items which require a certain amount of space, then you can calculate the minimum amount of space required.

A balance has to be struck between your current reality and your aspirations. It is unwise to invest in an impressive office building complete with fountain and atrium if you simply can't afford it. But in many businesses, it is important to be able to impress your customers, so a garden shed is probably unsuitable. 'Many companies mistakenly confuse the solidity of their premises with the solidity of the

> **"Many companies mistakenly confuse the solidity of their premises with the solidity of business, and proudly engrave their logos into the concrete of their pristine new corporate head offices."**
> Laurence Lyons

Where you work checklist

1. How much space do you need?
If you are opening a shop or factory you might have some idea of how many square feet your business requires. If you need an office think of how many separate rooms or how much floorspace you might need.

2. What needs to fit in?
What essentials have to be fitted in? These might be machines, displays, computers or other equipment.

3. What kind of premises do you need?

- ❏ an office
- ❏ a warehouse
- ❏ a factory
- ❏ a garage
- ❏ a shop.

4. Where are your customers, suppliers and competitors located?

- ❏ in a localised area
- ❏ dispersed throughout the country
- ❏ in large cities
- ❏ in rural areas
- ❏ abroad

5. Do you have in-depth knowledge or contacts in a particular area?
Can they help your business?

business, and proudly engrave their logos into the concrete of their pristine new corporate head offices. All this achieves is slightly to reduce the value of the building to the next tenant or purchaser,' says consultant Laurence Lyons.

If you are thinking of buying or renting an office, two factors should also be taken into account (as well as cost): the fundamental nature of offices is changing; and it could be possible to work at home rather than spending money on expensive office space.

● The death of the office

Among the huge and garish office blocks in Los Angeles is one which is unusual even by the standards of hip and bizarre LA. One-half of the building appears to be a ship, while the other *could* be a factory, and the two are joined by a gigantic pair of binoculars. The building is home to top US advertising agency, Chiat/Day. If the exterior is a little unusual, what goes on inside is even more unconventional. Chiat/Day is creating a revolutionary new working environment which may well be a prototype for the office of the future.

In a Chiat/Day office people will not have a desk, a telephone or a computer. Instead, they will have their own cellular phones and notebook computers. Nor will there be any need for filing cabinets – all documents will be saved in a computer network. Chiat/Day has long dispensed with the divisive walls and obsessive privacy of the conventional office. In the 1970s the company became open plan and now intends to replace this approach with an office organised around public meeting places.

The sceptical might suggest that what happens in a fashionable and trendy advertising agency in Los Angeles has little bearing on the office world elsewhere. They would be wrong. Offices are taking on radical new shapes and appearances as organisations come to terms with new technology and the increased expectations of customers and staff. This means that the old stereotype of an office is fast approaching extinction – except in television comedies where the sturdy desk, utilitarian chair and grey filing cabinet can still be seen (usually accompanied by an unused year planner, a pot plant and a family portrait).

As the pace of technological change continues at break-neck speed, the new world of the office is one of high-tech wizardry, colour and creature comforts – from being unadorned cells, offices now resemble a combination of computer salesroom, hotel lobby and conservatory. The talk is of ergonomics as well as economics. The simple things in office life can no longer be taken for granted. The humble desk is no longer sacrosanct. The desk of the average executive once had to simply bear a hefty weight of paper. Now, instead of in-trays, they are likely to carry a computer, printer, telephone and fax. They might also have a desktop videoconferencing system or the latest in desktop photocopiers.

Of course, the way offices look is closely tied up with the way people work. Changes in working practices are propelling offices towards the next century. The growing emphasis on teamworking, for example, means that desks are no longer set apart in glorious isolation, but grouped together. Indeed, as Chiat/Day is attempting to prove, managers don't necessarily *have* to have a desk. The office world is championing the idea of 'hot desking' – this means that people do not have a fixed place of work. Desks are regarded as corporate resources so people move from one to another depending on the task in hand.

While 'hot desking' is a fashionable term, it is nothing new – people like auditors and VAT inspectors have been doing it for years. And while it sounds attractive for companies, there is often a lot of reluctance among people to give up their desks. They like the security of working in the same place every day.

The emphasis on increasing productivity and efficiency among managers and office workers has led many major corporations to seek professional advice. There are a growing number of specialists whose services cover everything from carpeting to reconfiguring office layouts and buying the furniture. Companies are only now paying more attention to the cost implications of their offices. In the past, they tended to select a particular location without thinking about planning the office configuration, their furniture needs or even calculating running costs. The trouble with turning your office into an ergonomic triumph is the expense. The office equipment market is thought to be worth around £1.5 billion in the United Kingdom alone and the office furniture market adds many more noughts to corporate budgets. Smaller and less well-off companies are likely to blanche at the cost of bringing in interior designers to decide what colour of carpet will create the right atmosphere for their business.

There is no escaping the fact that offices are highly expensive. 'Take away the empty nights, weekends and holidays and you have an enormously expensive asset utilised for 21 per cent of the year – equivalent to 76 out of 365 days,' says Bruce Lloyd of South Bank Business School.[1] The trend, therefore, is for large offices to be abandoned as companies seek out flexibility – there were 250 planning applications in 1994 to switch properties from office use to housing in London alone.

The temptation is to regard the cost of your office in a different light from other business expenses. Businesses often fail to consider the level of return on their investment in office space. Research has shown that a maximum of only 5 to 10 per cent of an office building yields any return at all.[2] Often the real return is about one-third of this figure. Independent calculations from large organisations come to the same conclusions. Based on a total possible utilisation of 365 days a year, the figure is arrived at after making allowance for a five-day week, an eight-hour day, holidays, sickness, late arrivals and early departures. The time utilisation of office space clearly represents an appalling return on capital employed.

---

[1] Quoted in *The Guardian*, 14 November 1994
[2] B. Lloyd, 'Office productivity – time for a revolution', *Long Range Planning*, Vol. 23, No. 1, 1990

The true figures are probably even worse than this when space utilisation is also accounted for. Large portions of office buildings are often taken up with expansive reception areas. Many contain offices that are constantly unused. It is probably fair to say that the real utilisation of office space must often be in the region of single figure percentages.

Key questions

- Why do you need an office?
- Could you set up an office at home?
- Who will work in the office?
- Could they work at home?
- Who will visit the office?
- What do they expect to find?
- If you really do need an office how can you ensure it is fully utilised?

● The office at home

Working at home has one clear advantage: cost. There are no hidden extras ... apart from additional insurance to cover your business, probably extra heating costs and an extraordinarily high phone bill.

It is estimated that there are around four million people in the United Kingdom alone now working from home – a figure anticipated to rise to five million by the year 2000. It is little wonder that homeworkers are increasingly being targeted as a potentially lucrative new market. Alcatel's new 2592 Screen Phone, for example, aims to provide 'an extra pair of hands with no weekly wage' – it acts as an answerphone, address book and appointments scheduler, helpfully reminding you of your commitments with a preprogrammed message. Why employ an assistant when technology can do the job for you?

To many self-employed people, the idea of working at home appears very attractive. They fondly imagine themselves sitting on comfortable chairs reading the paper, popping upstairs occasionally to do a little bit of work. Reality may well prove a disappointment. The logistics of working at home can be complex.

Others are less enthusiastic. While numbers of homeworkers are growing, what is surprising is that so few people have actually taken advantage of technology to make the leap homewards. In theory at least, huge numbers of people could work equally efficiently at home, away from the distractions of the office. Yet people appear perversely addicted to commuting and there is still a strong attraction to the traditional office environment. They like the social side of going to work in the same place and meeting people face to face, rather than communicating by modem and fax.

While the culture of the office remains a considerable lure, there is also a great deal of suspicion of those who choose to work at home. Even if you accomplish far more, 'working at home' can be seen as a euphemism for avoiding work. How can you call sitting in front of the fire doing a bit of background reading work? What about all the distractions – the children, window-cleaner, telephone calls from gossiping relatives? And the temptations – reading the paper, watching the television, gardening, painting and decorating? In fact, anything rather than working.

Making the home office work

First, think about where you can work. Most people's houses aren't designed for office space. The last thing you want to do is to have to buy a bigger house to fit your office in when you are just about to find out if your bright idea makes business sense. Many people end up working in their dining room, bedroom or kitchen. This is a little awkward to say the least. It is difficult to hold meetings in a room filled with laundry or children. It is, however, not impossible.

Others convert garages, install sheds or other more elaborate buildings at the end of their gardens. A consultant I spoke to had converted his garage into a high-tech office complete with video-editing suite and sofas – 'Many of my customers are from big organisations. They like coming out here, sitting on the sofa and making themselves comfortable, they feel more relaxed in a different environment. There is no point in me trying to recreate the environment they are used to – it is simply too expensive.' So, when you are planning your office, do not try to turn your house into a corporate headquarters (even though on paper that is what it actually is). Be flexible and realistic.

In practice, the first rule of creating your own home office is to confine yourself. Decide on where you will work and tell everyone else in the house. Do not spread yourself round the house. If you do, you will soon find that children and pets have little respect for important pieces of paper. Other key factors are:

- ***phone lines*** It is useful, but not essential, to have a phone line which is dedicated to business use. This allows you to keep track of how much you are spending on business calls and may go some way to ensuring that passing adolescents or toddlers don't answer important calls with an indecipherable noise. An answerphone is now obligatory for virtually every business. You can't be at home all the time and an answerphone is a cheap and effective means of making sure you don't lose any business while you're out. Installing a new phone is comparatively easy – unless you want one right at the end of the garden. A dedicated fax line is also extremely useful and worth the investment.

- ***furniture*** The sky is the limit. But for a reasonable budget, you can find many second-hand bargains. The world is awash with ageing filing cabinets discarded by large companies on the advice of their interior designers. It is, however, not worth skimping on your desk and chair – your back will soon pay the cost.

- *filing space and shelves* Any business requires some sort of filing system. You need to make space so this can be done in an orderly way and so that important files are accessible.

● Using technology

The world's top business people have had a long love–hate relationship with the latest technology. Some simply can't get enough of the newest innovations. They pore through PC magazines, allow their eyes to glaze over at the very mention of an Apple Mac and constantly demand a larger budget to buy the latest version of their software package. Others remain sceptical – executive gizmos, they argue, aren't the route to increased profitability. Who needs IT when technology has yet to prove its commercial worth? And, they might add, what's wrong with the old-fashioned way?

To some extent scepticism is justified. Technology has not yet yielded the huge pay-offs promised. In the United States during the 1980s, $1 trillion was invested in Information Technology, innovations such as relational database technology, EIS, EDI and CAD. Amid the profusion of acronyms and the frenzied signing of corporate cheques, it was easy for organisations to forget or overlook the purpose of the investment.

Technology, whether it be a new software package, a portable computer, enhanced hardware or a new IT system, *should* lead to greater efficiency and productivity. Certainly, technology can bring you more receptive and accurate information and communication systems, and they can become closer to consumers, markets and each other. On the factory floor technology leads to faster, less labour-intensive and more reliable production. But statistics and extensive research from throughout the world suggest that productivity gains have not yet materialised. General Electric vice-president Gary Reiner has startlingly observed: 'We have found that in many cases technology impedes productivity.'

IBM chief Lou Gerstener, leading the computer giant back into profitability, has mapped out the expectations of the market with typical forthrightness. 'Customers have become very sceptical of the constant flood of new information technology. Customers are saying – give us technology we can manage, that is easy to use, that evolves at a reasonable pace and, most of all, helps us to achieve measurable competitive advantage.'

Of course, those who aren't true believers, are not the best people to spread the technological faith to others in the organisation. While primary school children can spot the difference between versions of Windows, chairmen of major corporations often find it difficult to sort out their modems from their mouse. But, in spite of suspicions and various pieces of research exposing the perils of technology, people in business can't simply opt out of the technological revolution. Opting out is the sure route to business failure.

> **Technology must add value, allowing people to work more effectively or to work in places where previously they could not.**

'In this business, by the time you realise you're in trouble, it's too late to save yourself. Unless you're running all the time, you're gone,' observed Microsoft's Bill Gates of the computer industry. The same is now true of virtually all business sectors. As a result, businesses are looking to technology to deliver tangible business benefits. The emphasis is shifting to technology which is practical rather than technology for its own sake. Technology must add value, allowing people to work more effectively or to work in places where previously they could not.

Mobile computers, for example, are rapidly growing in popularity. It is thought that the world market for portable computers amounted to six million units in 1993. Since then notebooks and, now, sub-notebooks have emerged as the latest means of working on the move. Growth of 20 to 25 per cent is anticipated in these markets during 1994. Technological advances mean that much of the processing power of an ordinary desktop computer can now be carried by a lightweight portable. A sub-notebook weighs in at around a kilogramme. There are even palmtops – Hewlett Packard's 100LX, for example, could be a constant companion and can call up Lotus 1-2-3 software at the press of a button.

Such technology was once pure gizmo, something to impress people with at dinner parties and on the golf course. Now it is geared towards practical use. The Psion Series 3 of handheld computers, for example, offers a number of new packages. The 'Banking Assistant' helps executive travellers keep track of expenses as they move from country to country and displays the results in a chosen currency. It also has a multi-exchange facility which allows five currencies to be used together. There are now also Timing, Sales, Data and Text Assistants.

To the self-employed such technology can be a major advantage. It allows them to do a huge number of tasks which they once had to be specialists to do, and they can effectively take their office wherever they choose. Laurence Lyons practises what he preaches and his home office makes the most of technology. 'A phone, fax and answering machine are essential and it is unlikely you can survive without a computer and a printer,' he says. The basics are backed up in Lyons' office by a modem, different printers, a laptop, access to CD-Rom, as well as the Compuserve network. 'You have to be careful not to become carried away. You have to think what value you add to your business by having a particular machine or service. Now, you can do a lot of impressive high-tech work with a minimal investment.'

Peter Chatterton, multimedia expert and author of *Technology Tools for Your Home Office*, thrives on the technological possibilities. He has an array of multimedia devices, including an Intel Desktop Video Telephony system which enables direct video links to clients via a camera on top of his PC, but points to the need to remember the basics. 'As a sole trader having an effective accounting software package is important – I use a very simple one, Money Manager from Connect, which I update every day. I can go to it and instantly find out what my bank balance is and when I need to pay credit card bills,' he says. 'Technology also means that I hardly ever write a letter – using e-mail is much cheaper than using a fax – and I also use Internet, Compuserve and Lotus cc mail gives me a direct line to the desktops of my clients.'

While specialists like Peter Chatterton are taking technology forward into entirely new areas others may blanche at the investment required. Keeping up to date clearly requires a great deal of money, and as a result there is now a booming second-hand market in computers and printers which, if you shop around, can produce bargains. The trouble is that bargains rarely come complete with guarantees and service agreements. What seems like a cash saver can soon turn into an expensive mistake. If there is no back-up, a single bug can bring the home office to a standstill.

Danny Miller runs his own Wokingham-based computer company. 'The key for anyone setting up their own office must be to use technology to gain control over their business. Technology is not about gizmos, but enables business people to control projects and finances and to communicate speedily and accurately. Forget these basics and you run the risk of buying equipment which you don't really need.'

Making information available to whoever needs it, wherever they are, sums up the way the market is developing. Technology has to make every facet of the solution practical. The trouble is that technology is moving forward so quickly that it is difficult to imagine any one person requiring or mastering the range of facilities available, even in a notebook computer. Typically, Apple's Newton can also log on to office electronic mail systems, send and receive faxes and talk to PCs. NEC's Versa E Series allows users to change their own hard disk, upgrade the memory, move from mono to colour display and includes 'an ergonomically designed trackball'. If necessary, Siemens-Nixdorf's PCD-4L (the 'Green PC') can even switch itself off to save wasting electricity. There is much, much more. This is the tip of a technological iceberg – in the business parlance it is 'added functionality'. Faced with such an array of possibilities, it is tempting for the self-employed to shrug their shoulders and stick to what they know works.

Instead, they should look at each piece of equipment in a number of ways.

- ***How does it bring you closer to your customers?*** One consultant bought all his major clients video phones. These were highly expensive, but his reasoning was simple: 'They probably don't know anyone else with a video phone, so the only person they can talk to is me. This makes them feel that I am part of their organisation.'

- ***How does it make your processes more effective?*** Technology must break down barriers, enable people to communicate easier and quicker.

- ***What if it goes wrong?*** You need full back-up and support. It is worth paying for.

- ***Who will use it and what skills will they need?*** There is no point having the latest technology if people can't use it effectively or to its full potential. This requires training. You can learn how to use a new computer system by thumbing painfully through the 500-page manual. But you would be better advised to go on a short course to get you quickly up to speed.

"**We've taken a company that was moribund and made it thrive, chiefly by refusing to squander our greatest resource, our people.**"

Ricardo Semler

6

People and your business

● The family comes too

No self-employed person is an island – family, friends and employees have to be looked after ... as well as yourself. Your family can be a vital ingredient in your success. Never underestimate their capabilities or forget about the impact self-employment is having on them. Not only are they affected by your change in working patterns and circumstances, but they may well be joint owners or a vital part of making your business work. It is estimated that over 85 per cent of small businesses in Europe are family-controlled.

> **"Your family can be a vital ingredient in your success."**

Trouble can come in a number of areas.

- **The family as investors**   If members of your family have financial involvement in the company, this can lead to arguments and divisiveness. You may be uncomfortable with the idea and they may appear to be interfering in the business's day-to-day running.

- **The family as workers**   The family are often helping hands. This is great, but you have to be careful you don't abuse their assistance. Treating them as unpaid lackeys is hardly likely to be conducive to harmonious family relations. Similarly, if your business continues to rely on unpaid helpers, its financial sustainability has to be questioned. It is one thing taking advantage of offers of assistance in the early stages, quite another when the business should be well developed.

- **The family as bystanders** At the other extreme, many families can feel excluded when you start your own business. It may be very exciting for you, but if you don't involve them they may well become less than enthusiastic. So, keep them up to date with what's happening and involve them wherever you can – without taking advantage of their natural willingness to help.

● People just don't understand

If you start your own greengrocer's shop, people can easily understand what you do and where. If, however, you work at home people, including family and friends, are notoriously slow at grasping exactly what you do and how. Their lack of insight or interest can seem hurtful, especially if you are taking a substantial risk in becoming self-employed. Among common comments are:

- **The astonished** 'What do you find to do all day?' Used to frittering away much of their time in traditional offices or spending hours commuting, people are amazed that you are busy doing something all of the time.

- **The sensible advice** 'I saw a job in the paper which would really suit you' Uncomfortable with the idea of you working at home, people are keen to set you up with a *proper* job.

- **The annoying** 'I thought I'd give you a call just for a chat ...' This is a common problem. If you work in a *proper* job, your relatives would not call up in the middle of the afternoon and expect you to be ready to chat about ailing aunties for an hour. If you work at home, it is assumed that you have plenty of time on your hands.

- **The patronising** 'You'll have to be neat and tidy for that meeting'. If you work at home you tend to dress casually.

People find it difficult to understand that when you have to be persuasive and impressively professional, you are capable of shaving and polishing your shoes.

● Managing stress

No-one ever said that becoming self-employed would be easy. People setting out in search of a less stressful existence can be disappointed. But very many succeed in reducing the amount of unnecessary and counterproductive stress in their lives. For those in work, stress is an endemic feature of their existence. A survey of nearly 1,000 managers by the Institute of Management in 1993 observed: 'The impact of stress is far-reaching. Three-quarters say it has some impact on their morale, on their effectiveness at work and on their relationship with their partner. Seven in ten believe their overall health is affected. Two-thirds suffer disturbed sleep patterns and around half are often unable to get a particular worry out of their head.'

The British Safety Council estimates that stress and stress-related illnesses cost £90 million in working days and £13 billion in absenteeism every year. American figures calculate that stress cuts GNP by 10 per cent through inefficiency and absences.

A 1994 survey in the United Kingdom found that more than half of white collar workers claim that stress has increased in the past two years and 16 per cent admitted it had caused them to take time off. In addition, 37 per cent did not feel appreciated at work and more than a third would not pick the same job again. The research was carried out by the amusingly entitled Associates for Research Into the Science of Enjoyment (ARISE). 'The nineties company is a lean, mean, stressful machine,' observed Professor David Warburton of Reading University. 'Most workers were led to believe that there would be a period of overwork in about 1992, and then they would go back to a period of normality. Now they find companies are downsizing and rightsizing and things are not changing: they are feeling more overworked.'[1]

Self-employment does not bring an automatic end to stress. Indeed, it can seem as if it simply produces a different type of stress. Among the most common causes of stress for self-employed people are:

- **Isolation and responsibility**   It's all down to you. There is no back-up. You are burdened with a heavy weight of responsibility from which there is no immediate escape.

- **Work and play are inseparable**   For those who work at home or live over their shop there is no escape. This can create problems on both sides as work trespasses into family life. Some sort of boundary needs to be established – make rules about working at weekends and evenings. Of course, these rules have to be flexible, but it is still worth having a few guidelines.

- **Money**   Without a regular assured salary, money worries are easily understood. To survive means that people need to be more pragmatic and flexible towards money. Poor cash flow is common to virtually every small business and is highly stressful. There is probably no way round it, so it has to be coped with.

- **Worry is constant**   You may land a big contract but, after the initial celebrations, your worries return – Will you be able to deliver? What happens afterwards? Are you putting all your eggs in one basket? Such concerns cannot easily be swept aside by blanket assertions that you are doing the right thing.

---

[1] *The Guardian*, 14 November 1994.

What stresses you?

Think of working in an organisation. What situations or circumstances cause (or caused) stress for you?

- [ ] Interruptions
- [ ] Unrealistically tight deadlines
- [ ] Pressure from your boss
- [ ] Competition from colleagues
- [ ] Unreliable colleagues
- [ ] Unreliable suppliers
- [ ] Pointlessly lengthy meetings
- [ ] Overload of work
- [ ] Firing people
- [ ] Hiring people
- [ ] Travelling to and from work
- [ ] Meeting budget targets
- [ ] Worries about job security

Do you think self-employment will bring the causes of your stress to an end? In all likelihood a number of these stress-inducing factors will be present in any business, but they are likely to be at a reduced level. And if it is your own business, you should be able to manage them more effectively.

- [ ] *Interruptions* Use an answerphone; give instructions that you will only accept certain calls; make it clear what people can and should interrupt you with.

- [ ] *Unrealistically tight deadlines* Agree to realistic deadlines; if you are struggling to meet them, keep the customer informed.

- [ ] *Pressure from your boss* Not if you are the boss; but remember how you felt, there is no point in pressurising people simply to exert your authority.

- **Competition from colleagues** Encourage teamworking; make it clear that your only competition is with competing companies, not with each other.

- **Unreliable colleagues** You recruit them so this is your responsibility.

- **Unreliable suppliers** Develop relationships with suppliers so that they, too, feel as if they are part of your team.

- **Pointlessly lengthy meetings** Don't allow them; make sure that meetings are organised, useful and brief.

- **Overload of work** Working 16 hours a day can mean that you are poor at delegating or need more staff.

- **Firing people** Take recruiting people seriously and invest time in finding the right person, then you may be able to avoid having to dismiss them.

- **Hiring people** A sign that your business is developing.

- **Travelling to and from work** Usually reduced, often eliminated.

- **Meeting budget targets** Set realistic, but challenging, targets.

- **Worries about job security** Simply replaced with worries about your business.

● Managing your time

Self-employment demands a large amount of self-discipline. Nowhere is this more evident than in managing your time. The temptation to avoid doing any work is often very strong. Working at home, for example, you might prefer to do a spot of painting, hoovering, read the papers or do the washing up rather than getting down to work. Sometimes you will be able to do so. On most occasions you have to get back to work – there is nearly always something that needs attention.

It is unlikely that you will work a 40-hour week. A common complaint among the self-employed is that work is often a case of feast or famine. As a result, you may find yourself working 100 hours during one week when you're deluged with work and only a few hours during the next when the work comes to an end. In many ways this sounds quite attractive – concentrated well-paid effort followed by a period of relaxation. In fact, it is far from satisfying unless you know that more work is imminent, rather than relaxing you will find yourself worrying about where the next job is coming from.

It is worth remembering that working by yourself is often more productive. If you work for an organisation there are a host of distractions, from gossip around the coffee machine to pointless meetings. Indeed, if you ring half-a-dozen people in large companies it is a fair bet that at least three of them will be in a meeting at any one time. The lack of such commonplace distractions means that, generally, the self-employed are highly efficient (and when it comes to meetings are keen to get on with the real business).

This is no great achievement when one considers life in an organisation. In the 1970s the Canadian management expert, Henry Mintzberg, spent time with five organisations and analysed how their chief executives organized their time. His book, *The Nature of Managerial Work*, revealed managers to be hostages to interruptions, flitting from subject to subject, rarely giving undivided attention to anything. 'The pressure of the managerial environment does not encourage the development of reflective planners,' Mintzberg observed. 'The job breeds adaptive information-manipulators who prefer the live, concrete situation. The manager works in an environment of stimulus–response, and he develops in his work a clear preference for live action.' Instead of being isolated figureheads analysing and generating carefully thought-out strategy, managers were suddenly exposed as fallible and human. They were rarely able to concentrate on a particular task for any length of time.

In contrast, the self-employed can exercise a greater degree of control over what they do and how they do it. Key to this are:

- ***Balancing administration with money-earning activities*** Efficiency does not mean spending all your time filing things neatly away. A balance has to be struck between the day-to-day administration of your business and activities which earn you money.

- ***Not seeking escape into non-essential tasks*** You have to recognise what you don't like doing whether it is making sales calls, doing your VAT returns or writing proposals. You can put some jobs off, but others have to be done regularly and efficiently if you are to run your business porperly.

- ***Planning ahead*** You need to try to be aware of when your busy periods are going to be and plan accordingly. If you know you are going to be busy next week, sort out your accounts now.

- ***Minimising time-wasting meetings, travel and pointless sales calls*** You need to evaluate how good a use of your time a particular activity is. Meetings can prove particularly wasteful. It may sound a good idea to have a weekly meeting with all your staff, but it is pointless if one person dominates or the phone keeps ringing. You have to make sure that everyone gets the most from meetings so that everyone thinks they are a good use of time.

You may also spend a lot of needless time travelling. It is a good idea to meet customers face to face, but in many instances other journeys could well be avoided. Use technology; send someone else; get them to come to you. Obviously sales calls are essential. But there is little point travelling 200 miles to meet someone who is not in a position to buy your product or service. You have to ensure that such visits really count.

- **Prioritising** You need to prioritise your actions. This is worth doing on a daily basis. At the start of the day, write down a list of things you must do today, could do today, and others which need to be done some time. You will have to continually decide what is the best use of your time. There is no formula. It is down to you to decide whether an hour's filing is better than an hour updating your customer base.

- **Telephone calls** Telephone calls can be the bane of your life. Every time you sit down to concentrate on something the phone rings and you spend ten minutes sorting something else out. Clearly, you have to take urgent or important calls. But if you work at home, use an answerphone to give you a chance to get some work done. If you are in an office, make it clear when you can't be disturbed and whose calls should be put through. When you are making telephone calls it is a good idea to do them in batches. Making four or five calls one after the other is far more effective than spreading them out through the day.

Read on

Gerard Hargreaves, Dorothy Morfett and Geraldine Brown, *Making Time*, BBC Books, London, 1993

- **Setting realistic targets for work and finance** Key to all of this is to be realistic about the targets you set yourself. If your 'to do today' list exends to five pages it is unlikely you will ever achieve it in a month, let alone a single day. Your targets need to be reasonable and achievable. Otherwise you will end up perpetually disappointed with your own performance. It is also worth remembering that jobs usually take longer than you anticipate. Build this into the time you plan to take.

- **Recording what you do** It is helpful, at some stage, to analyse how you spend your time. This could take the form of a diary for a week. This doesn't have to be incredibly detailed. You could just split your work into a number of categories:

- sales calls
- administration
- internal meetings
- finances
- customers.

Alternatively, you could identify money-earning and non-earning activities. Your week might look like the example opposite.

A week in your business life

Key
- [x] Non-earning
- [✓] Earning

Monday am
- [x] Team meeting to plan week ahead
- [x] Admin
- [x] Meeting with accountant

Monday pm
- [x] Sales calls
- [✓] Finishing small job for new customer

Tuesday am
- [x] Meeting with supplier

Tuesday pm
- [✓] Iron out delivery problems; talk to and reassure customer
- [✓] Negotiate new price with customer who wants quicker delivery

Wednesday am
- [x] Sales calls

Wednesday pm
- [x] Write proposal
- [x] Meeting with bank manager
- [x] Finish writing proposal

Thursday am
- [✓] Catch up on customer feedback telephone calls
- [x] Interviews for new assistant

Thursday pm
- [✓] Lunch with major customer
- [x] Check proposal before sending out

Friday am
- [✓] Meeting with plant manager to review work under way
- [✓] Call customer to discuss technical problem

Friday pm
- [x] Check monthly production figures
- [x] Talk through queries with management

As your business develops, how you spend your time will change. At the start you are likely to be involved in almost everything. You will deliver products personally, be closely in touch with each and every customer, know where every penny has been spent. As the business grows, this will change. You will find that you spend less and less time directly involved in the nitty-gritty. Instead, your time is likely to be increasingly taken up with administration and finances. Many self-employed people are happy with this. They are probably tired of being the van driver, salesman, stamp buyer and managing director.

For others this change is disturbing. They don't want to be administrators or accountants, they want to get their hands dirty or meet customers. The key to solving this problem must be to identify what you enjoy doing and what you are good at. If you don't have the attention to detail to go through the VAT returns, the likelihood is that you are not doing them as thoroughly as you should. You need to identify where your skills would benefit the organisation the most. You might, therefore, need to recruit a book-keeper or finance manager to look after the books while you spend more time with customers.

● Managing people

Managing people is a matter of trust and, increasingly, of developing and retaining talented people. In the past, trust was in short supply – you paid someone to do a job and paid someone else to supervise them. 'The microdivision of labour has fostered a basic distrust of human beings. People weren't allowed to put the whole puzzle together. Instead they were given small parts because companies feared what people would do if they knew and saw the whole puzzle,' says Charles Handy. 'Human assets shouldn't be misused.'

Managing people was once the means to an end. Now, it is much, much more. 'Twenty or thirty years ago companies talked of labour management. Later it was realised that knowledge and skills are important. Now it has gone a stage further,' says Philip Sadler, author of *Managing Talent*. 'Knowledge is hard to destroy; hard to protect; and hard to measure. But, the true source of competitive advantage is not so much knowledge as talent, which is the only remaining scarce resource.'

Developing talent

The idea of selecting the best people, rewarding them well and developing them for the future, is not something which rests easily with the British consciousness. Philip Sadler's research covered 50 leading international companies and American corporations, such as drugs company Merck and Hewlett-Packard lead the way. UK's ICL rated highly and others, such as British Airways, Glaxo and Unilever are also in the first division in the talent competition.

The British are still a little suspicious of those with talent while greatly admiring gifted amateurs who seem to take things less seriously. Elsewhere, there is a greater willingness to recognise and reward talented people. In Germany and France, for example, professionally qualified people have a much higher standing in society. But staying ahead of the competition is no longer simply a question of finding a neat niche or making things cheaper than anyone else. Such advantages are unlikely to last long anyway. They depend on having people talented enough to spot the opportunities in the first place.

'Some, perhaps most, organisations are totally dependent on identifying, nurturing and retaining talented people in order to survive,' says Sadler. 'The long-term success of the business in attracting, retaining, developing, motivating and utilising the best talent in its field is likely to be the biggest single factor in determining its long-term commercial viability.'

The research highlighted ten fundamentals for the successful management of talent:

- Provide a clear sense of direction and purpose
- Develop an appropriate organisational framework

- Understand your culture
- Identify future requirements for talent
- Develop recruitment and selection strategies
- Identify high potential
- Retain your talent
- Set clear objectives and ensure they are met
- Motivate and develop your talent
- Evaluate your talent.

> **"Talent is one thing, achievement is another."**
> Philip Sadler

Even so, part of the traditional distrust of human resource management has been that talent and knowledge are notoriously difficult to measure. Companies have often preferred to concentrate on logistics and productivity which can be more easily measured.

So what is talent? A merchant bank quoted in Sadler's book, describes talented people as 'intelligent, bright team players capable progressing and growing'. Another organisation defines a talented individual as one who knows the business, products and the markets; is extremely good at communication; has a winner's mentality; has drive; is able to operate in an ambiguous environment; has not just intelligence but social intelligence, able to understand human, political and bargaining processes; can take initiatives and sensible risks. Given this pot-pourri of skills, sorting out the talented wheat from the chaff is not easy. To find the right people, BA's recruitment operation handles 72,000 applications a year; 13,000 interviews; 159,000 unsolicited enquiries; as well as 10,000 people who walk in off the street.

Of course, having enlisted talented individuals, there is no guarantee of business success. As Philip Sadler says: 'Talent is one thing, achievement is another.'

Developing trust

The second vital ingredient to managing people successfully is trust. You have to trust them to do any job they undertake to the best of their ability and in a way that is satisfactory to what the company wants to achieve and how it should behave. When Ricardo Semler took over the Brazilian company, Semco, from his father he spent the first day firing 60 per cent of the company's top management. Almost without thinking, he had set in motion a revolution from which the rest of the business world is now anxious to learn.

Today, Semco is a unique success story. It has managed to buck Brazilian commercial chaos, hyper-inflation and recession to increase productivity nearly seven-fold and profits five-fold.

Walking through the door, visiting executives immediately notice that there is no receptionist. Everyone at Semco is expected to meet their own visitors. There are no secretaries, nor are there any personal assistants. Managers do their own photocopying, send their own faxes and make their own coffee. Semco has no dress code so some people wear jackets and ties, others jeans. But the Semco revolution goes far beyond this. 'A few years ago, when we wanted to relocate a factory, we closed down for a day and everyone piled into buses to inspect three possible sites,' recalls Ricardo Semler. 'Their choice hardly thrilled the managers, since it was next to a company that was frequently on strike. But we moved in anyway.'

Semco takes workplace democracy to previously unimagined frontiers. Everyone at the company has access to the books; managers set their own salaries; shopfloor workers set their own productivity targets and schedules; workers make decisions once the preserve of managers; even the distribution of the profit-sharing scheme is determined by employees.

'We've taken a company that was moribund and made it thrive, chiefly by refusing to squander our greatest resource, our people,' says Semler. He does not regard the transformation of Semco as a lesson to be emulated by other companies.

Instead, he believes it simply points to the need for companies and organisations to re-invent themselves for the 1990s. 'There *are* some companies which are prepared to change the way they work. They realise that nothing can be based on what used to be, that there is a better way. But, 99 per cent of companies are not ready, caught in an industrial Jurassic Park.'

The plea for businesses to become more democratic and humane is a familiar one. The trouble, Semler candidly admits, is that listening to people, accepting their decisions and inculcating people with the need for democracy is far from easy. 'The era of using people as production tools is coming to an end,' he argues. 'Participation is infinitely more complex to practise than conventional unilateralism, but it is something which companies can no longer ignore or pay lip-service to.'

There is still a substantial amount of scepticism about Semco's approach and achievement which Semler has recorded in an international bestseller entitled *Maverick!* Former BTR chairman Sir Owen Green commented after a public debate that Semler was 'not maverick; he's an eccentric'.

The mistake people make, says Semler, is assuming that Semco is some kind of role model. 'This is just one more version of how companies can organise themselves and succeed. Democracy alone will not solve all business problems. In fact, as we constantly see, nothing prevents autocratic companies from making money.'

It is little wonder that traditionalists among the management fraternity find Semler's message unpalatable. Managers are constantly appraised by Semco workers rather than a coterie of fellow executives, and they have to become used to the idea of accepting that their decisions are not sacrosanct. Semler seems to be adept at biting his tongue when decisions don't go his way and admits 'there are a lot of people at Semco whose styles I don't actually like. I wouldn't have recruited them but quite clearly they do their jobs effectively – otherwise people wouldn't support them.'

As part of Semco's revolution, Semler has to a large extent become redundant. The chief executive's job rotates between five people. Diminished power is clearly not something which fills him with sadness, instead it is confirmation that the Semco approach works. 'I haven't hired or fired anyone for eight years or signed a company cheque. From an operational side I am no longer necessary, though I still draw a salary because there are many other ways of contributing to the company's success,' he says. Indeed, Semler believes that what many consider the core activity of management – decision-making – should not be their function at all. 'It's only when bosses give up decision-making and let their employees govern themselves that the possibility exists for a business jointly managed by workers and executives. That is true participative management.'

Semler's book is already a massive bestseller in South America. Interestingly, it has also found a receptive audience in Japan – so much so that Semler's advance was the largest ever paid for a business book in Japan. More than 6,500 readers have written to him to find out more. But the sceptics remain, and Semler admits that it is too early to make cut and dried judgements about Semco's apparent revolution. 'Really the work is only 30 per cent completed,' he estimates. 'In the long-term, success will come when the system forgets me and becomes self-perpetuating.'

The lesson from Semco is that trust can boost your performance. It makes commercial sense. But how can you build up such trust?

- ***Give people the power to use their intelligence and expertise*** Allow them to solve problems and set high standards for the business and themselves.

- ***Allow and encourage people to make mistakes*** If people know they won't be shouted at and sacked on the spot for making an error in good faith, then they will take on extra responsibilities and, when they do make a mistake, they will admit it and learn from it.

- ***Share information*** You don't have to tell every person you employ every single financial detail. But by sharing information with employees, customers and suppliers you can help to build closer bonds and relationships. It is one thing sharing the good news when profits are up, quite another sharing bad news as profits plummet.

- **Keep it small** The world's biggest companies are now in contortions as they try to break businesses down into smaller units. They realise that the days of 10,000 people working away in a huge factory are past. The new emphasis is on vibrant, relatively small business units where people work in teams, aren't weighed down with bureaucracy or hierarchy and can make things happen.

- **Listen to what people say** Ricardo Semler disagrees with many of the company's decisions, but goes along with them because they have concensus. Many other managers pay lip-service to asking employees what they think. If what the employees say doesn't fit in with their thinking they ignore it. If you are to build trust, you have to listen and act.

- **Share your success** In good times it pays to spread the bounty. It may be your business but you depend on the people who work for you.

- **Eliminate pointless administration and hierarchies** Time and energy is wasted on administration which doesn't help anyone – let alone customers – and on shoring up power bases. You might like a nice spot in the car park while the others fight over a couple of spaces round the corner, but what does that say about your priorities?

Employing people: the paper work

There is more to employing people than developing their talents and encouraging trust. There is, inevitably, the nitty-gritty of paperwork and form-filling. As an employer you are responsible for deducting tax and National Insurance from the pay of your employees. Most employees pay their tax under the Pay As You Earn (PAYE) system. This simply means that the employer deducts the tax and sends it to the Inland Revenue Accounts Office every month (or every quarter if the payments are below a certain amount). Every year the employer has to give full details of the tax and amounts paid to the employee.

The PAYE Tax Office may be different from your own Tax Office. If you are planning to employ someone, contact the office and they will give you a PAYE reference number. When an employee joins, you send off his or her P45 to the PAYE Tax Office. They will then send you a starter pack with all the various forms and tables you need to fill in.

The Inland Revenue provides a great deal of information about employing people. The starter pack contains information on National Insurance contributions, sick pay and maternity pay. The DSS has a free Advice Line for Employers on 0800 393539. Also, if you wish to computerise your records, you can receive helpful information from:

Inland Revenue
Computer User Notes
Comben House, Farriers Way, Bootle
Merseyside L69 9EU

● Learning to delegate

Delegation has always been recognised as a key ingredient of successful management and leadership. But in the 1980s delegation underwent a crisis of confidence – managers were intent on progressing as quickly as possible up the corporate ladder, working 12 hours a day to succeed rather than delegating so that others could share the glory. In the corporate cut and thrust, delegation appeared to be a sign of weakness. But for the self-employed learning to delegate is a vital factor in allowing the business to grow. This may go against the habits of a life-time. Many people have been brought up to believe that running a business was all about controlling, commanding and planning. Now the emphasis – particularly in small businesses – is on coaching, leading and acting as a resource. Though there are some problems.

- It is hard to let go. When the business started you needed to do everything. You sell, meet customers, do the accounts, deal with the bank manager, clean the coffee machine, paint the buidling and virtually everything else. As the business develops so, too, must your role. You have to learn to let go.

- Everyone thinks they can and do delegate. People rarely admit to being poor car drivers, nor do they readily admit to being poor delegators. Try asking people who work for and with you what they think of your willingness to delegate?

Then analyse your approach to delegation. In answering these questions the golden rule to be remembered is that if you do something which someone else could do, you are preventing yourself doing a task which only you could do.

- *Do you only delegate straightforward or mundane tasks?* If you only delegate things which are either unpleasant, boring or which you now regard as beneath you, think of how this must make other people feel.

- *Is delegation a last resort?* Often people only delegate when they are so deluged with work that they cannot handle another task. Delegation is the last resort. Clearly, it is better to think about what you can and should delegate and to do so sooner rather than later.

- *Do you interfere with tasks you have delegated?* Often people delegate tasks and then interfere so much they might as well have done it themselves. This does not build any confidence in the person you have passed the job on to. If they have a problem they know you will be along in a couple of minutes to sort it out. If you delegate, you have to step back and let people get on with it. Often you will be delegating tasks which you can do easily or which you would do in a certain way. You have to be prepared for other people to find them harder and to accomplish them in different ways.

- ***Do you worry about how the tasks you have delegated are being carried out?*** As well as delegating a task you are also delegating responsibility. There is no point in delegating if it simply makes you worry even more. Delegate the worry.

- ***Do you take time to delegate – explaining things properly – or do you do it quickly without thinking?*** If you simply throw a file at someone and say 'Sort that out' you are not delegating in a productive way. The person left with the file is liable to wonder why they have it, what they need to do with it and, most importantly, why they should bother when you obviously aren't prepared to spend any time explaining things.

- ***Do you take the safe option?*** If you are too busy to do something the obvious temptation is to pass the job on to someone who is highly accomplished and can do the job. This minimises your worries, but is not always the best way to delegate. Instead, try a riskier strategy – but one which will pay dividends in the long term – and delegate jobs to people who haven't done them previously. This flies in the face of conventional wisdom, but if you take the time to give them the skills they need and are there to coach them (rather than to interfere) you are actually developing people while delegating.

- ***Do you give feedback?*** If people are to learn from the tasks you delegate, you have to give helpful and positive feedback. Criticism needs to be constructive.

Read on

John Payne, *Letting Go Without Losing Control*, Pitman, London, 1994

● Leading people

In a similar vein to delegation, leadership is one of the great intangibles of the business world. It is a skill most people would love to possess, but one which defies close definition. Ask people about leaders they admire and you are as likely to be told Gandhi as John Harvey-Jones, Ranulph Fiennes as Richard Branson. Yet most agree that leadership is a vital ingredient in business success and that great leaders make for great organisations.

'Broadly speaking there are two approaches to leadership. You can theorise about it or you can get on and do it. Theorising about it is great fun, hugely indulgent and largely useless. Doing it – or doing it better – is demanding, frequently frustrating and of immense value,' says Francis Macleod, former chief executive of the Leadership Trust. 'Those who want to change an organisation must be able to change people and in that process there is only one starting point that makes sense. Learning to lead oneself better is the only way to lead others better.'

The trouble is that what once constituted a great leader may not be the recipe for managerial success in the empowered 1990s. The leader's role has changed. It has become more complex and arguably even more critical to success. Leaders must ensure that high performance levels are achieved and sustained; handle complexity and ambiguity; enjoy leading the change process; ensure that the organisation and its processes constantly develop; and that people within the company are motivated, developed and rewarded to produce outstanding results.

The new business leaders have to be veritable Renaissance men and women. The very individualism associated with leadership is also now a bone of contention. The people we tend to think of as leaders – from Napoleon to Margaret Thatcher – are not exactly renowned for their teamworking skills. But these are exactly the skills that management gurus insist are all-important for the 1990s and beyond.

Delegating checklist

What tasks do you delegate?	To whom?	Why?	How do you collect feedback?

'In some cases, the needs of a situation bring to the fore individuals with unique qualities or values, however, most leaders have to fit their skills, experience and vision to a particular time and place,' says psychologist Robert Sharrock of YSC. 'Today's leaders have to be pragmatic and flexible to survive. Increasingly, this means being people rather than task-oriented. The "great man" theory about leadership rarely applies – if teams are what make businesses run, then we have to look beyond individual leaders to groups of people with a variety of leadership skills.'

Indeed, the pendulum has swung so far that there is growing interest in the study of followers. Once the humble foot soldier was ignored as commentators sought out the General, now the foot soldiers are encouraged to voice their opinions and shape how the organisation works. 'Followers are becoming more powerful. It is now common for the performance of bosses to be scrutinised and appraised by their corporate followers. This, of course, means that leaders have to actively seek the support of their followers in a way they would have never have previously contemplated,' says Robert Sharrock.

Phil Hodgson of Ashridge Management College has analysed a number of business leaders. His conclusion is that old models of leadership are no longer appropriate. 'Generally, the managers had outgrown the notion of the individualistic leader. Instead, they regarded leadership as a question of drawing people and disparate parts of the organisation together in a way that made individuals and the organisation more effective.' He concludes that the new leader must add value as a coach, mentor and problem solver; allow people to accept credit for success and responsibility for failure; and must continually evaluate and enhance their own leadership role. 'They don't follow rigid or orthodox role models, but prefer to nurture their own unique leadership style,' he says. 'And, they don't do people's jobs for them or put their faith in developing a personality cult.' The new recipe for leadership, says Hodgson, centres on five key areas: learning, energy, simplicity, focus and inner sense.

In contrast, traditional views of leadership tend eventually to concentrate on vision and charisma. The message seems to be that charisma is no longer enough to carry leaders through – leaders with strong personalities are as likely to bite the corporate dust (as Bob Horton found to his cost at BP). The new model leaders include people like Percy Barnevik at Asea Brown Boveri, Virgin's Richard Branson and Jack Welch at GE in the United States.

The magic which marks them apart has been analysed by INSEAD leadership expert Manfred Kets de Vries. 'They go beyond narrow definitions. They have an ability to excite people in their organisations,' he says. 'They also work extremely hard – leading by example is not dead – and are highly resistant to stress. Also, leaders like Branson or Barnevik are very aware of what their failings are. They make sure that they find good people who can fill these areas.'

In the age of empowerment, the ability to delegate effectively is critically important. 'Empowerment and leadership are not mutually exclusive,' says Professor de Vries. 'The trouble is that many executives feel it is good to have control. They become addicted to power – and that is what kills companies.'

"Business revolves around continuous relationships and links with customers, suppliers, stakeholders and employees wherever they may be."

⑦
Making your business work

● Developing your business

Making a business work is a delicate balancing act. For all the books on the subject, views on how to reach that balance remain as diverse as ever. Similarly, performance varies from business to business. Two businesses in apparently identical situations, selling the same products to the same market, may be performing totally differently. For the small business the challenges are formidable. The balancing act is highly precarious. For example, costs have to be kept down, but if you are too strict you might overlook the technology investment which is essential to your expansion. You have to develop your own skills, but there simply isn't the time to do so. There are many more such paradoxes.

The development of a business often follows this pattern.

Stage 1: Survival

This can last for up to two years and is the most testing time for the business and all those involved in it. At the beginning merely surviving from one week to the next is an achievement. Every new customer is a cause for celebration and every week of business a triumph.

Stage 2: Settling down

During this stage, concerns with merely surviving become secondary – though they linger at the back of your mind. Preoccupations with simply keeping afloat are replaced with an emphasis on consolidation and consideration of where to go next. The way forward can seem fraught with decisions and difficulties.

Stage 3: Development

Having weighed up the possibilities, the business now moves forward, seeking development in new markets or investing in new technology or buildings. This is the growth period. The business achieves a certain status.

Stage 4: Building the business and its people

A business which solely develops its products and services is liable to encounter problems. People, too, need to be continually developed. The emphasis during this stage, therefore, should be on building and developing new skills within employees and yourself. You may, for example, have to develop teamworking skills or improve your technological or mechanical skills. But bear in mind the crucial don'ts.

- **Don't move too fast**   Impatience is sometimes necessary but, in the early stages of building a business, it is more likely to cost you money than make it. Companies go bust often by moving too fast, trying to develop too quickly, without adequate financing or back-up.

- **Don't lose control**   Subcontracting or passing jobs on to someone else runs the risk of damaging the fragile fabric of your reputation if it goes wrong. You have to keep control, while still being flexible, responsive and quick.

- **Don't respond too slowly**   If a customer enquiry yields the response 'Our sales representative will be around to see you soon' your demise may be more imminent than you think. You need to respond with a firm date. No sales support means no sale.

Moving through these stages, avoiding these common pitfalls and making the business work is likely to involve some, if not all, of the critical elements which follow – and many more.

● Remember who you are in business for

There are a number of groups whose satisfaction is paramount to your continuing commercial success. Overlook any of them and your business is likely to encounter trouble.

- ***Customers, clients and consumers*** Is your business truly geared to their needs? To what extent is their input collected and implemented to ensure you give them what they want every time?

- ***Employees*** Are the human resources of the business put to the best possible use or is there a great deal of wasteful duplication of roles and responsibilities?

- ***Regulators*** There may be regulatory bodies whose activities are important to the company. Do you have relationships with any people or organisations which have a voice in forming regulations which might affect you?

- ***Suppliers*** How are suppliers involved in the company's systems and would increased involvement from them lead to greater efficiency?

- ***Yourself and your family*** Ultimately if the business is driving you towards a nervous breakdown or a heart attack, or driving your family apart, there is little point continuing. You should continually weigh up how the business is progressing from a personal perspective:

    ❏ Are you enjoying it?

    ❏ Are your family enjoying it?

    ❏ Are you developing your skills?

☐ How does it compare with what you did previously?

☐ Is running the business proving detrimental to your health?

> **Key questions**
>
> Ask yourself the following questions. These are not optional – any business needs to know the answers if it is to develop.
>
> - What do your customers expect from your business?
>
> - Do you consistently deliver what they want?
>
> - How do you know?
>
> - What do your employees expect and receive from the business?
>
> - What do your suppliers expect and receive from the business?

● Get close to customers

A national advertisement for Dell Computers reads: 'To all our nit-picky – over demanding – ask-awkward questions customers. Thank you, and keep up the good work.' Massively successful, Dell questions 20,000 customers every day. It realises that listening to customers and actively canvassing their opinions is a vital investment in the company's future – and not a costly indulgence.

The age of customers taking charge has arrived. Mass production is giving way to mass customisation. In the early part of the century, Henry Ford was quite content to produce a car in a single colour. Variation was expensive. Ford kept it simple and once observed, 'I've got no use for a motor that has more spark plugs than a cow has teats.' Now customers demand much more. When US aircraft maker Boeing asked its customers what they would like in the new Boeing 777, they requested it should have galleys and toilets which could be relocated anywhere in the cabin within hours. In May 1995 when the first Boeing 777 is produced the owners will be able to rearrange the aircraft within hours, configuring it with one, two or three passenger classes to fit the market at the time.[1]

The development of the Boeing 777 is an excellent example of an organisation being forced, through the growing competitiveness of its markets, to make basic changes in its approach. When it began developing the 777, Boeing recognised that it was lagging behind its competitors. McDonnell Douglas and Airbus had a substantial head start. 'We knew how to build aircraft but not how to operate them. We had to learn how to think like an airline,' says Boeing's Ron Ostrowski. Boeing radically altered its product design process. Instead of performing design and development tasks sequentially it began running them in parallel. Functions were displaced by design teams which also included customers. Ideas from a British Airways team, for example, helped the Boeing designers install an extra 12 seats making the 777 more attractive to potential customers.[2] By talking to customers and listening and acting on what they say, Boeing hopes to produce a product which is exactly right for its markets.

Customers want involvement, choice and the benefits the latest technology can give. Therefore, companies have to change their offerings quickly and frequently. This applies to nearly all businesses. If you are a greengrocer and there is a sudden rush on coconuts at your shop you will buy more. But it is just as important to find out why coconuts are suddenly popular. It may, for example, be linked to a cookery programme on TV. You may then be able to anticipate next month's popularity of dates.

---

[1] T. Peters, 'About turn on integration', *Independent on Sunday*, 5 December 1993.
[2] M. Wheatley, 'Boeing Boeing', *Business Life* December 1993/January 1994

Customers demand products which meet their needs, delivery when they want it and easy payment arrangements. This means that everyone in your business must be able to make operational decisions rather than mindlessly carrying out repetitive processes or giving standard answers or exhibitions of helplessness when facing customer queries.

Your business does not stop when the customer leaves after making a purchase or when a product leaves the factory. Business revolves around continuous relationships and links with customers, suppliers, stakeholders and employees wherever they may be.

Most companies assume that they know what their customers want. Few bother to ask more than the most basic questions about customer satisfaction. If and when they do, they are often surprised. Customers frequently have a unique and detailed insight into how their supplier works and organises itself.

South London plastics company Hunter Plastics found that its customers emphasised service and profits rather than, as Hunter assumed, price and quality. The market research prompted Hunter to develop closer relationships with its customers. Buyers from customers' organisations have subsequently visited the company's factory to discuss issues that concern them, and products have been developed to meet their requirements more accurately and consistently. The end result is that Hunter Plastics is now the single source of supply for some customers in particular product ranges.

It is easy to overlook the fact that in many businesses your customer is not the final consumer. If you make vases for shops, your ultimate customer is the person who buys a vase from the shop. So, remember your customer's customer.

Key questions

- Can customers contact you easily?
- Do they actually do so?
- Do you regard customers as individual people?
- How do you treat them as individuals?
- How many customers do you know by name?
- How quickly can you respond if a customer wants more information and help?

The customer is king, but ...

To the traditionalist, talk of customers being king might be difficult to take. If you are a specialist, highly trained and knowledgeable about what you do, what right has the customer to tell you what he or she wants? Such attitudes are common but ignore the fundamental truth that customers are not reliant on you; you are reliant on them.

But the customer is not *always* right. Even kings are allowed the occasional error. If you run a book shop and a customer requires a limited edition issue of a Slovak book which has to be imported and which would actually lose you money, you are unlikely to accept the order. The customer might suggest that you build up your selection of Slovak folk stories. As you are a specialist sports book shop this would be inappropriate. You might like to point to your one remaining copy of Slovak sporting heroes as evidence of your willingness to stock the best of Slovakia.

The customer is not always right, but you still have to listen to them and explain why you don't think they are right. They need to understand you as well as you understanding them.

Use technology to get close to customers

Increasingly technology is the key to sustaining the competitiveness of products and services. Small businesses often have poor access to modern/flexible technologies and, even if they have access, they are often incapable of making full use of the technology. This is caused by a variety of factors, including cost (high capital investment), the restrictions posed by premises and an anti-technology bias among business owners. But technology can be a vital weapon in forming partnerships with customers and in learning more about them. Databases, for example, enable marketing to be tailored and targeted to highly specific groups and market niches.

Retailers are particularly adept at making the most of all the information at their disposal and of rigorously collecting information continuously. The US mail-order company LL Bean has customer records which go back decades.

You can build a database by:

- asking people to write in for free products (a technique used by American cigarette companies)

- asking customers to fill out details so they can be kept informed of future promotions and sales

- membership cards – stores such as Office World and DIY chains now have membership cards which offer discounts and enable the company to track the purchasing habits of customers

- link up with other organisations – it is often worthwhile to share information with companies in related businesses or areas.

Once established, a good database can offer instant personal contact with customers. It is important, however, that the information on the database is continually monitored and updated. Poor information is counterproductive.

● Turn customers into advocates

Many companies remain studiously insensitive to the needs of their customers. We have all received poor service and, given the choice, usually try to avoid repeating the experience. If we go to a restaurant with poor food and slow service we are unlikely to return. Businesses often don't appreciate that their future existence depends on having the same customer come back again and again.

> *"Businesses often don't appreciate that their future existence depends on having the same customer come back again and again."*

Indeed, it is only in recent years that significant research has been carried out into the commercial advantages of transforming customers into advocates. 'The economic benefits of high customer loyalty are considerable and, in many industries, explain the differences in profitability among competitors,' concluded Frederick Reichheld of Bain & Company in a 1993 *Harvard Business Review* article.[3] He pointed to the example of credit card company MBNA, which calculates that a 5 per cent increase in customer retention grows the company's profits by 60 per cent by the fifth year. 'Building a highly loyal customer base cannot be done as an add-on. It must be integral to a company's basic business strategy,' argues Reichheld. 'Creating a loyalty-based system in any company requires a radical departure from traditional business thinking. It puts creating customer value – not maximising profits and shareholder value – at the center of business strategy, and it demands significant changes in business practice – redefining target customers, revising employment policies and re-designing incentives.'

---

[3] F. F. Reichheld, 'Loyalty-based management', *Harvard Business Review*, March–April 1993.
Copyright © 1993 by the President and Fellows of Harvard College. All rights reserved.

> ## How much is a customer worth?
>
> Imagine a new customer who buys one of your products every month or every year. How much is that business worth?
>
> Now, calculate how much the business is worth over five years.
>
> Finally, consider how much effort you have to put into retaining the customer. It is almost certainly a minute percentage of their spending potential.

No matter what your business, you want customers to be loyal, to return and to encourage others to buy from you.

One study of the American car market found that a satisfied customer is likely to stay with the same supplier for a further 12 years after the first satisfactory purchase. During that time, the customer will buy four more cars of the same make. To a car manufacturer, it is estimated that this level of customer retention is worth $400 million a year in new car sales.[4]

Clearly, building such a relationship also expands the traditional concept of the key components of marketing activities. While once these were centred on product, price, promotion and place (the four Ps), relationship marketing adds three crucial new elements – people, processes and proactive customer service. Customer service is no longer an added extra, but at the very heart of all of these activities.

Everyone in business has been told that success is all about attracting and retaining customers. It sounds reassuringly simple and achievable. But in reality, words of wisdom are soon forgotten. Once companies have attracted customers they often overlook the second half of the equation. In the excitement of beating off the competition, negotiating prices,

---

[4] *Business Week*, 4 April 1993.

securing orders and delivering the product, managers tend to become carried away. They forget what they regard as the humdrum side of business – ensuring that the customer remains a customer.

Failing to concentrate on retaining as well as attracting customers costs businesses huge amounts of money annually. It has been estimated that the average company loses between 10 and 30 per cent of its customers every year. In constantly changing markets this is not surprising. What is surprising is the fact that few companies have any idea how many customers they have lost.

Who are your top five customers?

	Now	One Year Ago	Next Year
1			
2			
3			
4			
5			

Only now are organisations beginning to wake up to these lost opportunities and calculate the financial implications. Cutting down the number of customers a company loses can make a radical difference in its performance. Research in the United States found that a 5 per cent decrease in the number of defecting customers led to profit increases of between 25 and 85 per cent.

Rank Xerox takes the question of retaining customers so seriously that it forms a key part of the company's bonus scheme. In the United States, Domino's Pizzas estimates that a regular customer is worth more than $5,000 over ten years. A customer who receives a poor quality product or service on their first visit and as a result never returns, is losing the company thousands of dollars in potential revenue (more if you consider how many people they are liable to tell about their bad experience).

Increasingly the emphasis is on building relationships with customers to create loyalty so they return time and time again. Creating customer loyalty can appear relatively simple. Everyone who buys a Land Rover Discovery, Defender or Range Rover receives a telephone call or a postal questionnaire checking what they think about the product they have just bought. This is hardly earth shattering, but gives customers an opportunity to voice their opinion and makes it clear that there is more to the customer–supplier relationship than a simple purchase.

In the car market, customer loyalty has long been recognised as a vital ingredient in long-term success. Research in the United States showed that a satisfied customer usually stays with the same car manufacturer for 12 years, buying another four cars within that time. Not suprisingly, buying a car now guarantees a steady deluge of information and sales literature from the car maker as they try to ensure that you are not tempted elsewhere.

Programmes to increase customer loyalty are now all around us. If you are driving, they can be seen at every petrol station. In the United Kingdom they are long established. The simple purchase of petrol is not really affected by price. Left to their own devices, customers would stop at the nearest petrol station and fill up. Customer loyalty programmes make it a more complex matter. The first petrol station might offer points to be used at Argos for which you have already collected ten partly filled cards; another might offer tokens (collect 12 and you get a baseball cap); and so on. The choice is endless and, peculiarly, has become part of our culture. People still talk about Green Shield stamps, treasure the football coins they collected in 1970 and drink from wine goblets (free with 25 tokens in the mid-1980s).

The logic behind nurturing customer loyalty is impossible to refute. 'In practice most companies' marketing effort is focused on getting customers with little attention paid to keeping them,' says Adrian Payne of Cranfield University's School of Management and author of *The Essence of Services Marketing*. 'Research suggests that there is a high degree of correlation between customer retention and profitability. Established customers tend to buy more, are predictable and usually cost less to service than new customers. Furthermore, they tend to be less price-sensitive and may provide free word-of-mouth advertising and referrals. Retaining customers also makes it difficult for competitors to enter a market or increase their share of a market.'

Professor Payne points to a ladder of customer loyalty. On the first rung, there is a prospect. They are then turned into a customer, then a client, supporter and finally, if the relationship is successful, into an advocate persuading others to become customers. Developing customers so they travel up the ladder demands thought, long-term commitment and investment.

Customer loyalty programmes cover a multitude of activities from customer magazines to vouchers and gifts. Basically, a customer loyalty programme aims to persuade a person to use a preferred vendor in order to take advantage of the benefits on offer, whether a trip to Acapulco or a price-reduction voucher for a calorie-controlled can. Sceptics may mutter that there is nothing new in this. Indeed, businesses have been giving long standing customers discounts and inducements since time immemorial. What is different now is the highly organised way in which companies are attempting to build relationships and customer loyalty.

The process can begin even before the potential user is born. Nappy manufacturers are a prime example of companies which take a long-term view. Prospective parents are bombarded with sample packs, free information and literature about what will be best for their soon-to-arrive son or daughter. By the time of the birth, the parents already have some degree of loyalty to a company whose product they have never actually bought. It can seem excessive, but one nappy company estimates that a sales increase of a single per cent would pay for its entire customer loyalty programme.

Nowhere is customer loyalty more highly thought of than in the airline business. It has become a key differentiating factor. Invented in the early 1980s, frequent-flyer programmes are now well established and expanding rapidly in Europe where BA established its scheme in 1991. The beauty of the programmes is that the concept is simple and relatively cheap to administer. Programme members earn 'points' or 'miles' with every flight which can be redeemed for free tickets or upgrades to business class. Virgin's Freeway programme is a little more imaginative and offers hot-air balloon trips, flying lessons and visits to health clubs. The programmes mean an airline attracts and retains customers at a marginal cost while filling empty seats. The only down-side is for the companies who actually pay for the travel – they get the bill while their employees receive the perks.

Though the idea is simple enough, frenzied competition means that airlines are continually changing rewards and rules to outdo others in the market. Earlier in 1994, for example, British Airways doubled the number of points available for those who took a flight before a certain date; BA and American Airlines, keen to boost the lethargic German market, offered triple points to German travellers; Scandinavian Airline Systems offered business-class passengers starting from the United Kingdom a free overnight stay in a Scandinavian hotel; and Alitalia announced a similar scheme for flights from Italy to London.

This sort of feverish activity is not unusual. Clearly, frequent-flyer programmes work. One survey estimated that a quarter of Europe's business air travellers decide on their carrier because of frequent-flyer points. Carlson Marketing Group estimates that there are 32 million frequent-flyer members in the United States clocking up huge amounts of free travel. American Airlines' AAdvantage scheme claims 16 million members.

From the point of view of the airlines, frequent-flyer programmes offer the treasure at the end of the marketing rainbow: information. Airlines have historically been starved of information about their customers because only 15 per cent book direct with the airlines – the vast majority use travel agents and other sources. Frequent-flyer programmes give airlines priceless competitive information so they can target their marketing more accurately and really focus on particular market segments.

Technology means that customer loyalty programmes are becoming ever more sophisticated. When it comes to creating loyal customers, the database is king. When nappy makers introduced trainer pants to the United Kingdom they were relying on the power and accuracy of their databases to steal a march on their rivals. Procter & Gamble, Kimberly-Clark and Peaudouce each has a database which identifies families with children of potty-training age. The families were then deluged with special offers and various other inducements – Procter & Gamble's Pampers brand helped its publicity campaign along with an achievement chart ('I can poo in my potty' being the primary goal).

Databases mean that companies can target audiences more effectively. A DIY chain, for example, has a discount card which entitles holders to an annual payout – which comes in the form of a voucher to be spent at the shop. The details of the cardholders enable the store to send out regular mailings to customers giving them advance warning of special offers and giving them an extra 5 per cent discount on certain days.

Technology also means that one customer loyalty programme tends to blend into another. Take someone travelling on business. They decide to fly with Swissair to boost their points. They might then transfer to Delta which has a reciprocal arrangement with Swissair. Having clocked up the maximum number of points, on arrival at their destination the manager surveys the massed ranks of car rental companies and plumps for the one with an agreement with the airline. They then drive to an hotel in an international chain which also offers discounts.

'The cycle is never ending with loyalty to one product or service being bolted on to another,' says management consultant and author Tim Foster. 'The rapid expansion of customer loyalty programmes is proof that if they are well thought-out then they can have a great impact. If they are poorly constructed, the effect can be disastrous.'

Some come dramatically unstuck. A leading airline recently withdrew from the Australian market. This left thousands of angry Australians stranded. They had faithfully collected points on the airline's frequent-flyer programme and, unless they paid to fly to Hawaii, had nowhere to put the points to use. The airline's reputation has been damaged, probably beyond repair. Hoover's offer of free flights to the United States is perhaps the best known disaster of recent times, costing the company tens of millions of pounds and senior executives their jobs.

As with any kind of promotion or marketing activity there are risks attached to customer loyalty programmes. They can also be expensive. Producing a glossy magazine for customers throughout the world is far from cheap. Companies have, therefore, to carefully balance potential pay-offs with the actual cost of the programme. In fact, putting the simple idea into practice has become increasingly complex. Customers are now more highly demanding and fickle than ever before. They are organised and use their lobbying power more effectively. Expectations are high, but companies are quickly realising that customers with a conscience create new markets.

Companies are now developing loyalty programmes which are directly related to the conscience of their customers. There are a plethora of products which pledge to donate money to help save the rain forests or support medical research, if you buy them. A supermarket chain, for example, gives customers vouchers which they can take to their children's schools to save up for a computer. Such loyalty building creates a situation in which all sides appear to win – though, of course, the supermarket wins the most through creating a loyal customer.

Customer loyalty programmes are likely to become ever more ambitious. The potential for mutually beneficial link-ups is never ending. A credit card from General Motors would have been unthinkable a few years ago. Now it is the tip of an expanding iceberg. Some American supermarkets already give customers a 'smart card' which means the company knows the contents of each customer's weekly shopping basket.

From Green Shield stamps at service stations to smart cards at supermarkets, customer loyalty programmes have come a long way. They have never been so personal, but whether they succeed in creating customer loyalty is something which only time will measure.

● Become partners with suppliers

Suppliers are often as similarly neglected as customers. It is increasingly recognised that organisations are missing a major opportunity – it has been estimated that companies spend around 50 per cent of total production costs on suppliers. The Chartered Institute of Purchasing and Supply estimates that some businesses could be spending up to a third more than necessary on suppliers.

The entire process of building closer relationships between customers and suppliers has become known as **partnership sourcing**. Its origins lie in large multinationals buying supplies from smaller companies. Companies like Glaxo, Kodak, IBM, Nissan and British Airways, for example, are all champions of the approach. Computer company ICL has nearly 200 suppliers signed to its vendor accreditation scheme. The programme arose from analysis which showed that of 6,500 suppliers, ICL did 70 per cent of its business with a mere 200. Suppliers in the accreditation programme have to achieve high quality standards and are subject to performance evaluations by ICL. They are also expected to link up directly with ICL's electronic trading system and, increasingly, to deliver components directly to the production line. ICL's relationships are such that it shares research and development and formulates joint marketing strategies with its leading software supplier.

As in so many instances, Japan is a rich source of best practice. Toyota, for example, manufactures only a third of its needs in-house. It calls on 300 contractors who are at the top level of its tiered supplier structure and who work closely with Toyota. They are also members of its product development teams. The top tier of suppliers then contract out much of the work to smaller suppliers. All the way down the supplier chain, companies are linked by their recognition that working together is a situation which benefits all sides.

A 1993 survey of 280 of the leading European companies by consultants Booz, Allen & Hamilton found that 60 per cent of those interviewed insist on a regular presence at their suppliers, compared with 40 per cent five years previously. The consultants anticipate the figure will soon rise to 75 per cent. In addition to this, companies are reducing their supplier base at more than 3 per cent a year, a figure which Booz anticipates will double. BA, for example, had 10,000 significant suppliers in the 1980s – a figure which has now been reduced to 3,500 and is set to fall further. Booz's research suggested that the best performing companies are those moving to 'lifetime' agreements or long-term contracts with suppliers. Interestingly, the best also appear to make the most of fewer resources. In many cases the smaller the purchasing department, the more impressive the performance in terms of material costs, material quality and inventory turnover.[5]

The attractions of partnership sourcing are persuasive:

- adversarial relationships between buyers and suppliers are replaced by ones of mutual support and benefit
- large companies can keep costs down by committing themselves to buying greater amounts from smaller suppliers
- the customer–supplier relationship can be one of mutual learning with both sides benefiting from an external and new perspective on their business

---
[5] T. Dickson, 'A source of best practice', *Financial Times*, 20 August 1993

- product development is more likely to match customer needs if the customer's business is more fully understood by the supplier

- product development is likely to be faster.

It is also worth noting that partnerships are more likely to prosper between organisations which have shaken off narrow functional approaches. An organisation which finds it difficult to communicate quickly and effectively internally is unlikely to be able to manage a successful relationship with an outside organisation of any sort, especially one that can seem, to the traditionally-minded, intrusive.

'In a partnership it is unlikely that both parties will have equivalent power,' says Roger Pudney of Ashridge Management College, who has carried out extensive research into customer–supplier partnerships across the world. 'But, both parties should be bringing something very distinct to the relationship which the other partner needs. Traditional adversarial type relationships lead companies to exercise their power to gain advantage over their competitors, suppliers and customers; in more collaborative relationships this attitude has to be put to one side.'[6]

● Keep it simple

KISS ('Keep it simple stupid') is a useful acronym to bear in mind. Some of the biggest companies in the world have built their success round this idea. They frown on diversification into markets they know nothing about and on tinkering with something which has proved itself successful. Why shower customers with unnecessary choices when all they want is a straightforward product of high quality at a decent price?

As businesses grow there is a strong temptation to provide added extras, to make the product or service more complex and therefore, you think, more appealing. This is often the route to disaster. Change the product and you run the risk of

---

[6] R. Pudney, 'The power of partnerships' *Directions*, September 1993

annoying the very people who have made you successful in the first place – customers.

Moving into completely new areas carries huge risks. Some of the biggest corporations in the world have made major errors in moving into businesses they knew next to nothing about. Diesel engine-maker Cummins moved into ski resorts; Letraset bought stamp dealer Stanley Gibbons; Coca-Cola bought Columbia Pictures; Hawker Siddeley bought a distillery. The list of companies which thought they could transfer their expertise into other businesses and failed is a lengthy one. For the small business the risks are even greater – they have everything to lose. If you have set up a successful window cleaning business do not be tempted to move into ladder manufacture.

The answer to many of these potential pitfalls is to keep it simple. This sounds straightforward but the temptation to add extras in an effort to boost sales is strong. Henry Ford is renowned for his ability to keep it simple – Model Ts remained black after all. In fact, Ford was undone by the fact that he kept it simple and the same. It is one thing retaining a straightforward aim and an idea of why you are in business, quite another to become stuck in a rut. The message is keep it simple and change constantly. 'Businessmen go down with their businesses because they like the old way so well they cannot bring themselves to change,' said Ford, neatly summing up his own failings.

McDonald's is a great example of what can be done. It is constantly changing what it offers its customers – there are special promotions, combinations of products and occasional new products – but it doesn't change too much. You know what you will get. You know there will always be a Big Mac, fries, shake and apple pie. McDonald's changes but stays the same. Indeed, it changes to stay the same.

● Commit to quality

Quality was the management phenomenon of the 1980s. It is here to stay. Quality is now expected. Your products and services must meet the increasingly high quality standards of customers. But quality is not about relentless supervision, looking over people's shoulders to ensure they are doing a high quality job. Quality seeks:

- ***to eliminate waste*** Waste comes in many forms: products which simply can't be used and have to be discarded; the cost and time spent correcting or repairing poor quality products; the customers which are lost because of poor quality levels. According to one estimate from the DTI, 25 per cent of an average company's turnover is wasted on poor quality.

- ***to offset waste*** The traditional response was to *check*, but checking is also expensive. Companies employed supervisors and quality controllers simply to identify the waste generated in the first place through poor quality. By the time the checkers have got to the problem it is generally too late; the product is made.

I have just ordered a table from a national chain. It is a simple table but the delivery time is four weeks. I asked whether I could just buy the one in the shop. This was unthinkable. And instead of delivering the table directly to my house, the shop plans to telephone when it receives it. I can then go into the shop and check it is the right table. They will then deliver it to my house. This process is cumbersome, but typical, and actually turns the customer into a checker.

Quality replaces the emphasis on waste and checking with systematic approaches to avoiding the problems in the first place. In the past a production line produced products which were inspected. Now attention is being paid to the people and the process at the very start. If they are better trained, have better equipment and are given more power they can save on waste and eliminate the need for checking.

Many small businesses are naturally quality conscious and have no need (or the money) for costly checking. They pride themselves on their personalised high quality product or service. The trouble now is that for many of their customers this is not enough. They want their suppliers to have proof that they are quality organisations. Small businesses are increasingly expected to have a quality accreditation such as BS 5750. If a small business wishes to expand into a new market it may well find that the only stumbling block is that it has to go through the rigmarole of achieving a quality label, even if it is already a high quality company.

There is a great deal of controversy surrounding the issue of standards for quality. BS 5750 is the most often cited business quality standard, but its deficiencies are often commented on. Currently this standard is not appropriate to the typical small business with its informal, hands-on approach to management and quality control. The Forum of Private Business estimates that an average small business owner spends about a third of his or her time working alongside employees, knows customers and they know the quality of the product. Such business people don't need the rigid and formal process of BS 5750 (which has now been renamed BS EN ISO 9000). However, obtaining a quality standard can be an important statement to your customers that you are committed to quality products or services. If you choose not to achieve such a standard you have to prove that you are quality conscious in other ways.

● Watch the competition

Too often businesses ignore the people who spend their lives trying to put them out of business – competitors. In practice you need to be comparing the way your competitors do business and how they perform financially against your own performance. If you don't learn from them, they might well be learning from you. Among the factors you should consider are:

- **Market share** Is the market share of your competitors changing? How is it different from your own?

- **Turnover** Are there means by which you can discover the turnover of your chief competitors?

- **Profitability** Are there means by which you can discover the profitability of competitors? Look at annual reports, press cuttings, tell your sales people to keep their eyes and ears open.

- **Key customers** Do you know the main customers of your competitors?

- **Service** How does the service provided by your competitors differ from your own? Could you offer similar or better service?

- **Products** Get hold of some of your competitors' products and examine them. How do they differ?

- **Marketing approaches** How do your competitors market themselves?

There is a great deal of publicly available information about other companies. Every limited company is incorporated and must lodge statutory documents at Companies House. Copies are available for inspection at offices in Cardiff, London and Edinburgh. Information may also be obtained from offices in Manchester, Leeds, Birmingham and Glasgow. If you are unable to visit the offices you can order a search by post, telephone or fax. This will give you more details about the companies.

Further information

The offices of Companies House are:
Cardiff Telephone: 01222 380801 or 388588
London Telephone: 0171-253 9393
Edinburgh Telephone: 0131-225 5774
Manchester Telephone: 0161-236 7500
Birmingham Telephone: 0121-233 9047
Leeds Telephone: 01532 338338
Glasgow Telephone: 0141-248 3315

Spread the burden

It can't all be down to one person

The dominant managerial problems facing small business management are often rooted in the psychology, technical calibre and business aspirations of the owner/manager and development of the organisational structure and management style.

Work as a team

What is a team? Is a team simply a fancy word for a group of people? What is the difference between a team and a task force? What is the difference between a team and a committee? Is a team simply a group of people with different skills aiming for the same goal?

Despite the extensive literature about teams and teamworking the basic dynamics of teamworking often remain clouded and uncertain. Teams only occur when a number of people have a common goal and recognise that their personal success is dependent on the success of others. They are all interdependent. In practice, this means that in most teams people will contribute individual skills, many of which will be different. It also means that the full tensions and counter-balance of human behaviour will need to be demonstrated in the team.

It is not enough to have a rag-bag collection of individual skills. The various behaviours of the team members need to mesh together in order to achieve objectives. For people to work successfully in teams, you need people to behave in certain ways. You need some people to concentrate on the task at hand (*doers*). You need some people to provide specialist knowledge (*knowers*) and some to solve problems as they arise (*solvers*). You need some people to make sure that it is going as well as it can and that the whole team is contributing fully (*checkers*). And you need some people to make sure that the team is operating as a cohesive social unit (*carers*).

Teamworking: who's who?*

Solver
Role Helps the team to solve problems by coming up with ideas or finding resources from outside the team. Can see another way forward.
Characterised by innovation, ideas generation, imagination, unorthodox, good networking skills, negotiates for resources.

Doer
Role Concentrates on the task, getting it started, keeping it going, getting it done or making sure it is finished. Some may focus on only one aspect of the task. Making sure it is finished is the most rare.
Characterised by high energy, high motivation, push others into action, assertiveness, practical, self-control, discipline, systematic approach, attention to detail, follow-through.

Checker
Role Concern for the whole process, tries to ensure full participation while providing a balanced view of quality, time and realism.
Characterised by prudence, reflection, critical thinking, shrewd judgements, causing others to work towards shared goals, use of individual talents.

Carer
Role Concern for the individuals in the team and how they are developing and getting along.
Characterised by supportive, sociable, concerned about others, democratic, flexibility.

Knower
Role provider of specialist knowledge or experience.
Characterised by dedication, standards, focus.

*E. D. A. Obeng, *All Change!*, FT/Pitman Publishing, London, 1994

For people to work well together you need both a range of specific skills or technical skills and a range of different human behaviours. When you look hard at people and how they behave when they are working in teams, you find that in addition to the actual content of the work they are doing, they take on certain behaviours. Each person has a favourite way of behaving when they work with others.

Modern management thinking suggests that you need a balance of behaviours for any change management activity. But you may wish to slightly unbalance the team in favour of the type of change you are trying to undertake.

It is also worth noting that for all the research which has been carried out into effective teamworking, teams remain a law unto themselves. Managers who sit down and play at human engineering by trying to select exactly the right sort of combination usually end up in a state of confusion. Often the teams that have worked in re-engineering programmes have come about spontaneously or include an unusual combination of specialists. The key to success does not appear to lie in the selection of team members – you only have to look briefly at team sports to find examples of talented individuals working poorly as a team. Instead, success is often characterised by the genuine granting of power and responsibility to teams so they can solve their own problems.

● Use experts

The small business owner/manager is often a strong believer in the marriage of ownership and control. This can lead to a failure to seek out or use technical specialists when they are required. Duties are not given priorities and strategic decisions may be overlooked in order to complete routine jobs. The lack of management specialisation creates inefficiencies and disadvantages in the innovation process (i.e. marketing tactics, design/development of new products/services and technological progress). In family businesses the management function tends to improve with the introduction of a new generation of entrepreneurs. Consider using experts such as:

- *accountants*
- *auditors*
- *lawyers*
- *financial advisers*
- *management consultants*
- *specialist consultants*
- *management trainers*

Using consultants

Much maligned, consultants can be an important source of expertise with objective views on your performance. Discovering the right consultants for you is difficult. There are an increasingly large number to choose from. You might come into contact with consultants through word-of-mouth (e.g. other people in the same professional network who have used consultants to do similar projects to the one contemplated); advertisements placed by consultants in newspapers, trade journals, etc.; direct marketing approaches by consultants; consultancy registers (a variety of organisations maintain registers of approved consultants and are happy to give information and advice concerning their selection). Having made contact you should look for:

- *the quality of response* Do they seem to understand your business and its particular problem? Do they ask questions and try and get under the skin of the business?
- *track record* Have they done similar work in the sector and when was the work performed?
- *the experience of others* Can you contact other businesses who have used the consultants?
- *is it clear what they plan to do?* You need to know

what the end-result will be – a report, recommendations or just an appraisal of the company?

- ***who will you be working with?*** Consultants may sub-contract work or use other colleagues who you haven't met. Ensure that you know who will be handling the work.

- ***costs*** Find out exactly what you will be paying for and when.

● Develop systems and processes

As you grow, the business becomes more complex. This demands that management practices change. When it was just you running the business from your home it was okay to have files strewn across the floor in organised disorder. When other people are involved, you can't afford not to have effective systems which people will have access to and make their jobs easier.

Quality guru J. M. Juran believes that 80 per cent of problems encountered in organisations can be put down to systems and the remaining 20 per cent to people. In small businesses this is especially true. Often prices, costs, marketing, quality control, inventory and strategic management are run on a whim rather than through an established process. Direct experience and informal management practices frequently prove to be adequate and compatible to the narrow resource base of small firms. But in some industries, small business management is characterised by deficiencies which adversely affect other business functions, especially during times of market turbulence, and when business growth demands more managerial expertise and administrative support.

What are the systems and processes in your business?

'It is not products, but the processes that create products that bring companies long-term success. Good products don't make winners; winners make good products,' say James

Champy and Michael Hammer in their bestseller *Re-engineering the Corporation*.[7]

If a company divides itself along product lines few eyebrows are raised. A building society, for example, divided its operations into separate businesses in the 1980s. These included mortgages, life policies and credit cards. Though it appears to be a logical thing to do, the trouble is that the fascination with products overlooks customers who are not so easily separated. A single customer may take out a mortgage and a life policy and want another credit card. They would prefer to be able to do so from a single entity rather than being passed from one product division to another.

The faith in good products leading to competitiveness is long-established. Yet time and time again innovative products have failed to yield the anticipated financial results. Other companies quickly copy them or produce their own versions of the product. With time-cycles diminishing, this is more efficiently done than ever before. Organisations can no longer rely on a new product reaping huge dividends over a lengthy period as competitors try and make up the lost ground. Products are now easily copied and retain their uniqueness for a shorter and shorter time.

In contrast, processes are more robust competitive weapons. They are unique to a particular organisation and, as such, are virtually impossible to copy. The trouble is that understanding and utilising that uniqueness is not easy. Understanding processes fully is time-consuming, complex and involves negotiating the maze of corporate politics and functional strongholds. It involves finding out who does what, where, why and with what impact on your stakeholders.

If you think about a task which forms an important part of your work you will quickly see what a minefield process analysis is. Consider a few basic questions:

---
[1] J. Champy and M. Hammer, *Re-engineering the Corporation*, Nicholas Brealey, London, 1993.

- *Why do you do the task?*
- *Where do you do it?*
- *When and for how long?*
- *Who else is involved in completing the task?*
- *Who does the task affect inside your organisation?*
- *Who does the task affect outside the organisation?*
- *What resources do you use to complete the task?*
- *What information do you need to complete the task?*

Any task you do can be looked at in terms of time, people, resources, information, internal users and external users. In addition, there is always a hefty dose of personal relationships, politics and sensitivities.

Complex though process analysis clearly is, at its heart is a straightforward idea. A process has been defined as 'any activity, or group of activities, that takes an input, adds value to it, and provides an output to an internal or external customer'. Alternatively, a process can be seen as a group of activities which cause change to happen through the execution of a number of simultaneous tasks. The change and the processes are in line with the organisation's goals and aligned, as closely as possible, to the needs of your stakeholders.

There is nothing mysterious or startlingly original about processes. All businesses have processes and they are a concept which people easily understand. The trouble is that people may not recognise the fact that their activities form part of a process.

Mapping out a process

So that you can find weak links and places where the process could be speeded up or improved in other ways, it is worthwhile writing down a process map. This is basically a list of the events and who is involved, in sequence. Identification of a potential customer might have a process map like this:

Action	Who is involved
Find address of potential customer	Salesman
Call to find name of individual	Salesman
Enter name and details on database	Salesman
Write sales letter	Salesman
Follow-up phone call	Salesman
Meeting with potential customer	Salesman and managing director
Write proposal	Sales team and managing director
Follow-up meeting	Salesman
Contract drafted	Lawyers and managing director
Contract signed	Managing director and customer
Production	Production team
Delivery	Production team and driver
Follow-up call	Salesman
Customer feedback put on database	Salesman
Customer invoiced	Accounts
Customer pays	Accounts

Think of a process in your business. Write it down in a similar way, detailing the actions required and by who. Obviously if you are just starting your business the likelihood is that the personnel will be yourself and yourself only. Looking at the process map are there any areas where:

- *the customer could become confused dealing with too many people?*
- *information is gathered and not used?*
- *the process could miss a step and be improved?*
- *improved technology would make the process quicker and easier?*
- *there is a pointless functional divide between who is involved?*

If you identify any blockages in your process map, you should be able to act to remedy them. Now you can draw up a map of what the processes should look like. Again, specifiy each particular task and who is involved. Then, underneath this, write a list of what needs to be done to achieve your new process map. You might need to improve your database, or involve more people in drafting proposals, or give a single person responsibility for handling a particular customer all the way through the process.

● Develop skills

As the business develops the skills of people must also develop. If, for example, you move into internal markets, different skills will be needed – at a basic level you might have to learn another language. So your own skills and those of employees must be continually enhanced to meet the changing needs of customers and markets. This is something often overlooked in the small business. The owner tends to regard investment in training and development as a luxury expense. But as the firm expands in a fast-changing environment, managerial skills become more important than operational or production considerations. The company has the expertise to produce products, but often it doesn't have the managerial skills to make the most of its knowledge.

In particular it is important that businesses:

- **Learn from mistakes**   'Because many professionals are almost always successful at what they do, they rarely experience failure. And because they have rarely failed, they have never learned how to learn from failure,' says Harvard Business School's Chris Argyris. If you don't learn from your mistakes you will continue making them.
- **Create opportunities for learning**   You have to make the time and finance available.
- **Support learning**   Encourage others to develop their skills.

● Recruit people professionally

Small businesses are notoriously poor at recruiting the right people. Commonly, the business owner recruits people who he or she likes. Usually they are similar in many ways to the business owner themselves. The end-result is a collection of like-minded clones who are all individually proficient but as a group are too similar to work effectively.

Effective recruitment requires a number of features.

Search effectively

There is a temptation to take the easy way out by hiring someone easy to hire rather than the right person for the job. You desperately need a new marketing manager. Funnily enough someone has just sent you their CV and it mentions some involvement in marketing. You immediately ring them up and invite them in. You lean back and contemplate another problem easily solved.

In fact, it is unlikely that the details on your desk are of the ideal person for your company. You have to be a little more systematic. You might go to a recruitment company, which will be able to give you a clutch of CVs very quickly, or you might activate some of your contacts in the business to see who is actively looking for another job or is unhappy where they are. The ideal person may walk though the door or, indeed, be a close friend or relation; but in all likelihood you will have to go and find them.

Don't make snap superficial judgements

As the candidate enters the room you may notice their unkempt appearance, stains on the tie, battered old suit and soleless shoes. But they may be the most brilliant computer programmer this side of Silicon Valley. While you must expect some people to look professional – or to dress in a certain way – you cannot make generalisations on how you expect people to look. You can, of course, insist that everyone wears blue suits and white shirts, but that doesn't make them any better at their jobs. You need to appreciate and value the importance of difference.

Interview, don't make a presentation

Potential recruits do need to know something about your company and the way it works. However, interviews need to be a two-way process. It is one thing giving essential information about your company, quite another to give a lengthy presentation on its values and culture.

Find out more

CVs are notoriously superficial documents. It is important that you use interviews to find out more about people. Try and find more about the real person behind the scant details of qualifications and work experience. Go beyond the facts.

Think to the future

The temptation is to hire someone who is a specialist who can begin work in a particular area immediately. In fact, it is often preferable to recruit someone who is flexible, adaptive and responsive, someone who can be developed into roles which are important to the company, rather than someone who has a narrowly defined set of skills which he or she refuses to deviate from. This is particularly important in a small business where all roles will undoubtedly overlap (and if they don't they should) to a greater or lesser degree.

● Seize the opportunity

At the beginning of the century, William Hoover was a manufacturer of leather goods especially for horse-drawn vehicles. Unlike many others, he recognised that the car would put him out of business. Coincidentally he was shown a prototype of a cleaner. He made several and managed to sell them. In 1908 he set up the Electric Suction Sweeper Co and produced 372 sweepers. Soon Hoover's product and name became known throughout the world – as did the company's slogan 'It sweeps as it beats as it cleans'.

Hoover could have carried on making things which the world increasingly didn't need, but was foresighted and brave enough to move into a completely different market with an untested product. For the small business, seizing the opportunity is vital to success. They can never stand still or become complacent.

High tech company Cumana was highly successful in the 1980s. Its chief customer was BBC Acorn which had quickly established itself in UK schools. Of the company's £4 million turnover, £3 million was accounted for by Acorn, In one year this collapsed – the £3 million became less than £1 million. Cumana eventually wrote off nearly £500,000 worth of stock. The lesson must be: look ahead and spread the risk.

Julie Dedman was made redundant, without warning, by the animal feeds producer she worked for. It was a blow made all the more bitter because only weeks before she had turned down a job offer from a rival company – she had been told that her job was safe and her work highly valued. 'It shook me so much I knew that I couldn't let anyone else have control over my life again. I had to work for myself,' she says. Her experiences galvanised her into action. She soon set up her own company, West Riding. Now, eight years on, it employs 13 people and has a turnover of £5 million.

Julie Dedman's idea was to offer dairy farmers a complete milk testing service which identified any infection or adulteration in the milk and come up with a solution. 'The only competitor was the Ministry of Agriculture. They were set in their ways and weren't giving farmers what they really needed. It was then a question of having the determination to go through with it. Redundancy does affect your confidence but you simply have to rise above it.'

Even when times are hard, there are opportunities – but only if you are prepared to find them. Greg Wong is a man who likes living dangerously. At the height of the recession, when the UK furniture industry in general was at a low and the office furniture sector particularly miserable, he went out shopping. What he and his partner, Dinesh Kanadia, came back with was not a set of office chairs, but a group of companies which they plan to transform into major contenders in the office furniture market. The result was the Mines & West group with a turnover of £8.5 million – an estimated 450 per cent improvement on the previous year's figures. Wong bought the venerable but troubled Mines & West manufacturing company when it was at its lowest ebb. 'Naturally many people would have considered it a rather unusual move to buy up a company in receivership in such a recession,' says Greg Wong. 'But here was an opportunity for an entry into a manufacturing industry that was really low. If I had started up a factory like Mines & West from scratch it would have cost a fortune.'

Wong believes that companies like Mines & West had got into difficulties through becoming carried away when the times were good. 'During the boom time in the '80s when demand for office furniture was high, loads of companies took on higher rents and extra staff. And what happened? The market shrank 20 per cent in a very short time leaving them all stranded with extra unused capacity.'

His solution is to specialise. 'Our strength, unlike other groups which try to be all things to all men and diversify their activities, is that we are solely manufacturers of furniture. That is what we intend to stay doing.' He believes that his strategy of cautious and planned growth with strong management support has already paid off. 'When we bought these companies they were all in receivership, Now each one is showing a £2 million turnover. In fact, one had not seen a profit for ten years and in the first three months after acquisition we put it into the black.'

What causes business failures?

The Official Receiver lists the common reason for businesses to fail:

- not enough capital
- not selling enough
- bad management
- taking too much cash out of the business too early
- poor accounting
- lack of experience
- bad debts
- setting prices too low
- growing too quickly and running out of cash
- fraud
- operating costs getting out of hand
- poor supervision
- competition
- health problems of the owner.

● Develop and use networks

Networking is not just about recognising the connections we have with others, it is also making the most of these connections. It is something we can all do, all of the time. We have the opportunity to make connections with each other whenever we talk, through face-to-face conversations, meetings or telephone calls, and whenever we write – through letters, internal memos, E-mail, proposals or reports. Networking can add value for us as individuals and also contribute to the results of our organisations. Among networks of particular use to the small business are those with:

- other businesses and business people
- suppliers
- business organisations – such as Chambers of Commerce
- professional bodies – such as the Institute of Engineering.

The business owner must utilise these networks fully. Often they can lead to increased business contacts and more business.

● Make the most of publicity

Newspapers and magazines have a lot of space to fill and are constantly on the look out for good stories about innovative business ideas and business successes. Small businesses are poor at taking advantage of this particular marketing channel. Commonly they suppose that publications are simply not interested in the activities of a small company or that publicity costs money, after all larger companies pay huge amounts of money to specialist public relations companies.

The lure of column inches is simply explained. Publicity means that your name becomes known. Favourable publicity may well attract customers. A mention in an article can produce sales leads (particularly if it has a contact number).

Consultant and author Tim Foster is highly adept at utilising publicity to get his name better known. 'I developed an idea of building a database of advertising slogans – slogos. So I started collecting them and when I had several hundred, proposed to *Marketing* magazine a weekly competition called 'Name that Brand'. In this, we'd list 10 slogos and 12 possible brands and invite people to match them up,' he says. 'This has led to the formation of a business that checks slogos for advertisers – Foster's Database of Slogos. Having my name in each issue helped me to build my own credibility and led to more business.'

As Tim Foster shrewdly realises there are a host of opportunities to gain coverage. Think first of what journalists could write about:

- **Your product or service**   Is your product or service innovative in any way? Is it new or new to your particular area or the country?

- **Your company**   Is there anything unusual about the way you work or organise things?

- **People**   Human interest stories are perennial favourites. Do you have an interesting story to tell about setting up the business?

- **Opinions**   Setting up a business may have convinced you of the inadequacy of financing arrangements for small businesses, perhaps your local paper would be interested in covering your views.

- **Events**   With what local or national events does your product or service have a link? If you make cricket bats, publications might be interested in writing about your company when the cricket season begins.

Read on

Tim Foster, *101 Ways to Get Great Publicity*, Kogan & Page, London 1993

Publications are looking for 'angles'. There has to be a point of topical, human or general interest for them to latch onto. It is largely up to you to provide it. You may seek out publicity in a number of areas:

- **Local newspapers** If your market is primarily local, this is a key medium for your business. It should be comparatively straightforward to be featured in articles.

- **National newspapers** You need a stronger story to reach the national press. It has to be highly topical or have some sort of general, national interest element. You may also like to develop a peculiar personal habit – such as eating hamsters for breakfast – which guarantees press attention, but is unlikely to boost your business.

- **Trade magazines** If you are selling to a particular business market, you need to look at the trade or professional publications to see what kind of material they are looking for.

- **Magazines** There are a growing number of business and management magazines which are particularly interested in case study-like stories usually along the lines of how you successfully took on foreign competitors, introduced total quality or achieved phenomenal success.

● Go for it!

As was emphasised at the beginning of this book, starting and running your own business is never going to be easy. It takes a huge variety of skills and, like a juggler, you have to deal with a huge range of different issues and problems all at the same time. If you take your eye of one of the balls, the whole lot are likely to cascade to the floor, taking you with them. But as more and more people become self-employed and seek out more flexible ways of working, awareness is increasing of how small businesses work and the assistance they often need. Support mechanisms are growing in number and in their usefulness – whether they are DTI grants, counselling for those made redundant or information from banks. The world is wakening up to the desire of huge numbers of people to set their own agenda and create their own brilliant careers.

If you have worked through the steps in this book and are acquiring the skills you will need to run your own business you are taking a step in the right direction – and into the unknown. If you are already running your own business, you now know the full range of issues and challenges which you face – now and in the future.

In the end success is down to you, the individual. You have to set demanding standards and be ambitious while still being realistic. You have to aim high, but at the same time keep your feet firmly planted on the ground and learn the lessons if you don't meet exacting targets. Forging a brilliant career will never be a *proper job*. **Go for it!**

Index

A

accountancy software, 124
Alliance of Small Firms and Self-Employed People, 63
American Airlines, 184
Ansoff, Igor, 88
Ardilles, Osvaldo, 73
Argyris, Chris, 203
Ashbridge Management College, 74, 168, 189
Association of Independent Businesses, 63

B

Bain & Co, 179
Barnevik, Percy, 169
Bates, Alan, 101
Boeing, 175
Bono, Edward de, 38
Booth, Hubert, 47
Booz, Allen and Hamilton, 188
Branson, Richard, 23, 71, 72, 169
British Airways, 157, 184
British Franchising Association, 60
British Safety Council, 147
British Venture Capital Association, 113
BT, 2, 20
Business Links, 62
business plan, 83
Buzan, Tony, 45–6

C

Capital Exchange, 113
Carlson Marketing Group, 184
Carlson, Chester, 54
Carnall, Colin, 74
CB Designs, 53
CCN Business Information, 23
Cedar International, 2
Champy, James and Hammer, Michael, *Re-engineering the Corporation*, 199
Chartered Institute of Patent Agents, 41
Chatterton, Peter, *Technology Tools for Your Home Office*, 140–1
Cleaver, Sir Anthony, 6
Coe, Trudy, 7
communication, 80–2
Companies Registration Office, 58

Coutts Career Consultants, 10
Cumana, 205
customer loyalty, 179–87

D

decision making, 75–80
Dedman, Julie, 205–6
delegation, 163–5
Dell Computers, 174
Department of Employment Small Firms Division, 61, 113
Department of Trade and Industry (DTI), 61–2, 110
Diner's Club, 39
Domino's Pizzas, 181–2
Drew, Richard, 54
Drummond, Robert, 73–4

F

Ford, Henry, 23, 174–5, 190
Forte, Charles, 23
Forum of Private Business, 62, 67, 123
Foster, Tim, 14, 86, 186, 209
franchising, 58–60
Frequent Flyer Programmes, 184

G

Gates, Bill, 139
Gerstener, Lou, 139
Giggs, Ryan, 11
Green, Sir Owen, 160

H

Handy, Charles, 2, 15
Hanson, Lord, 69
Harris, Bill, 10–11
Heinz, Henry, 23
Henley Centre for Forecasting, 16
Henley Management College, 74
Hewlett-Packard, 129
Hodgson, Jane, 97
Hodgson, Phil, 74, 168–9
Hoover, William, 205
Hornby, Frank, 70
Howe, Neil, 37–8
Hunter Plastics, 176

I

Inland Revenue, 8–9, 14–15
Institute of Independent British Business, 63
Institute of Management, *Managers Under Stress*, 5–6, 7
Institute of Manpower Studies, 23
Institute of Practitioners in Advertising, 96
Institute of Small Business, 63
intuition, 71–5

J

JCB, 112
Jeffes, Jonathan, 100
Juran, J. M., 198

K

Kaplan, Bob, *Beyond Ambition*, 101
Kroc, Ray, 42

L

Ladbrokes, 2
Laker, Sir Freddie, 72
Langdon, Ken, 84
leadership, 166–9
Leadership Trust, 166
limited company, 57–8
Linnell, Clive, 107
Lloyd, Bruce, 134
Lyons, Laurence, 132, 140

M

McDonalds, 42, 190
Macleod, Francis, 166
McLeod, Sally, 20
McNamara, Frank, 39
Majaro, Simon, *The Creative Gap*, 44–5
marketing, 90–6
Marshall, Sir Colin, 69
Microsoft, 139
Miller, Danny, 141
Mines & West, 206
Mintzberg, Henry, *The Nature of Managerial Work*, 151
Mistral, Georges de, 39

N

National Association of Shopkeepers and Self Employed, 63
National Federation of Enterprise Agencies, 4, 104, 106
National Health Service, 20
National Insurance, 116
NatWest, 62
negotiating, 96–9

O

Obeng, Eddie, 38, 107, 195
Observer, The, 4, 104, 106
obsession, 99–101
O'Donoghue, Denise, 103
Onassis, Aristotle, 39

P

partnerships, 56–7
Pascale, Richard, 15–16
Patent Office, 41
patents, 41
PAYE, 162–3
Payne, Adrian, *The Essence of Services Marketing*, 183
Pentacle, 38, 107
Peters, Tom, *Liberation Management*, 99
Poutziouris, Panikkos, 90
Procter & Gamble, 184
Pudney, Roger, 189
Purves, Sir William, 69

Q

quality, 191–2
quality standards, 192

R

Rank Xerox, 181
Reichheld, Frederick, 179
Reiner, Gary, 138
Roddick, Anita, 23, 111–12
Royal Insurance, 2

S

Sadler, Philip, *Managing Talent*, 157–8
Scott, Tim, 101
selling, 82–90
Semco, 159–62
Semler, Ricardo, 159–62
Sharrock, Robert, 74, 168
Simon, Herbert, 76–7
Sinclair, Sir Clive, 54, 72
Smof, Juliet, *The Overworked American*, 5
sources of support, 110–13
stress management, 147–50
suppliers, 187–9
Swatch, 42–3

T

tax, 113–16

Tec Invest, 113
Thorpe, Chris, 20
3i, 2

U

UK Venture Capital Journal, 113

V

Value Added Tax (VAT), 117–18
venture capital, 111–13
Vries, Manfred Kets de, 169

W

Wadlow, Derek, 37
Warburton, David, 147
Weight Watchers, 39
Widetch, Jean, 39
Withers, Gary, 71–2
Wolfson, Lord, 69
Wong, Greg, 206
working at home, 135–8

INDEX 215